The
Prayer Book Guide
to Christian Education

The Prayer Book Guide to Christian Education

THE EPISCOPAL CHURCH
The Seabury Press • New York

1983
The Seabury Press
815 Second Avenue
New York, N.Y. 10017

Printed in the United States of America

Library of Congress Cataloging in Publication Data

Episcopal Church.
    The prayer book guide to Christian education.

    "Companion guide to the Book of Common Prayer" —Introd.
    Bibliography: p. 14
    1. Christian education—Text-books—Anglican.   2. Episcopal Church. Book of
common prayer.   I. Episcopal Church. Book of common prayer.   II. Title.
BX5875.E64 1983   207   82-10820
ISBN 0-8164-2422-5 (pbk.)

Scripture quotations contained in the text are from *The Revised Standard Version of the Bible*, copyright © 1946, 1952, second edition of the New Testament copyright © 1971, by the Division of Christian Education of the National Council of the Churches of Christ in the United States of America.

Contents

Foreword

The Bible, being our principal written source for the religious education of Christians of all ages, is complemented by the Book of Common Prayer and the Hymnal. Add the logical custom of commemorating the events and words of the Lord Jesus in the liturgical sequence of the church year, and a pattern or outline for a curriculum in Christian education emerges. Give to imaginative and sensitive Christians the contents of the Bible, the Book of Common Prayer, and the Hymnal, and they can work out a program of Christian education for a whole congregation.

The obstacle, problem, or difficulty for many has been a lack of knowledge or experience in gathering, relating, and scheduling the related materials. This book provides a way of integrating and using these resources. It presents a key to the Prayer Book way of Christian development: an exposition of the Prayer Book guide to Christian education, a means by which teachers may learn and learners teach, evangelists may preach and hearers may truly hear—the better to lead, the more faithfully to follow in the way of Him who is the Truth and the Life.

May the Holy Spirit, the giver of all good gifts, so lead us in the way to share our gifts that all may come to the truth and live. So I pray in faith, commending this book to all who are disciples of our Lord Jesus.

+ JOHN MAURY ALLIN
23rd Presiding Bishop

Introduction

OUR HERITAGE AND TEXTBOOK

To be an Episcopalian is a way of being a Christian, a Christian with a special set of tools. First among these is *The Book of Common Prayer*. This is our unique heritage, and one we happily share with others. *The Book of Common Prayer* is a manual for worship, and as such is both the statement of what we believe and our call to ministry. It offers a flexible format for present-day worshiping communities, yet links us securely to our history and traditions; it is a handbook of faith and action. *The Book of Common Prayer* is a primary textbook for Christian education in the Episcopal Church.

Christian education is everything and anything happening anywhere that helps the Christian community grow in its life in Jesus Christ and in witness to him. Christian education includes our whole congregational life, everything we do as a family. For children and adults Christian education includes preaching and hearing, teaching and learning, and sharing in liturgy. Christian education includes what we do outside our church buildings, how we relate to our environment, how we offer our arts, how we share the Story, how we build relationships and grow in love with those around us.

WHO ARE THE EDUCATORS OF CHRISTIANS?

At the ordination of a bishop the candidate is asked, "Will you boldly proclaim and interpret the Gospel of Christ, enlightening the minds and stirring up the conscience of your people?" (BCP page 518) This responsibility is not solely the bishop's. It is also shared by rectors, who are charged by the Canons "to be diligent in instruction. . . ." The directions for Holy Baptism declare that "Parents and godparents are to be instructed in their duties to help the new Christians grow in the knowledge and love of God. . . ." (BCP page 298) During the service the entire faith community joins in pledging to "do all in your power to support these persons in their life in Christ. . . ." (BCP page 303) Then together they accept both personal and corporate responsibility for Christian nurture by affirming and renewing the Baptismal Covenant (BCP pages 304–05) and by welcoming and receiving the newly baptized into the household of God. (BCP page 308)

Very clearly, Christian education is a network of mutual responsibility for doing a ministry in which all persons, both laity and clergy, share. It happens locally, within a congregation or within a family. There is growing and learning throughout our lives, with possibilities as limitless as God's grace. Teachers and learners become interchangeable as people of all ages discover together to what they are called, to whom they belong.

We are shaped by secular liturgies, to which we are exposed day in and day out in family patterns and in myriad social forms. We must see the liturgy of the Church as consistent with what we believe, so that everyone in the faith, young and old, experiences welcome, care, and love. How liturgy is done has an important impact on Christian education of which congregation leaders need to be aware. Worship and education must be coordinated and drawn together at every possible juncture.

WHO CAN USE THIS BOOK?

This companion guide to *The Book of Common Prayer* is intended to gather in one place information and counsel for living, learning, and engaging everyday life issues through the cycle of the Church Year. Therefore, this book is for those who have responsibility for planning or teaching in the Church, and for all who share in liturgical services:

- clergy
- teachers and directors of education
- lay readers
- altar guild members and sacristans

- organists and music directors
- writers of parish bulletins and newsletters
- women and men in the pews
- families who study at home.

The guide is for use along with the Bible and the Hymnal. Some of the material may already be familiar, but other resources, including those in the list of ''Suggested References,'' offer more detailed information when it is needed. It is hoped that from this raw material programs meeting particular needs can be molded according to local creativity and imagination.

THE CHURCH YEAR: FRAMEWORK FOR CHRISTIAN LIVING

We live by many calendars—social, seasonal, civil, personal. The rhythm of our experiences and commitments shapes each of us and provides a context in which we can search for meaning in our personal lives, in our relationships with God and others, in work and play, in joy and pain, in our very living and dying. The Church Year gives us as Christians this same opportunity. At every point the focus is upon what God has done in Christ for all people in all ages, including us in our own day. In remembering and celebrating our Christian heritage we are drawn into the salvation story, to encounter and ponder, to proclaim and show forth Jesus Christ, who is ''the same yesterday and today and forever.'' (Heb 13:8)

Season by season, feast or ordinary day, the Church Year is like a bright jewel turning in the sunlight, whose facets reflect light and hold it for a time so that we may see more clearly within the unity the many splendors, joyful and contemplative, of what it means to share Christ's life on earth. Each repetition of season and feast holds the possibility of our seeing something new, a fresh surprise, which can illuminate our understanding and bring us to deeper faith and commitment. The Church Year gives us, as it has given Christian people throughout the ages, a way to live with Christ so that every year becomes The Year of Our Lord. So we mark our calendars *Anno Domini,* and with ''those in every generation in whom Christ has been honored'' we ''pray that we may have grace to glorify Christ in our own day.'' (BCP page 386)

CONCERNING THE LEARNING PROCESS

Every encounter is an opportunity to teach and to learn. The minute we sit down together we are involved in education. Whenever we start to plan we must be in touch with other persons sharing common concerns. We need to ask where what we are planning fits within the overall plan of the congregation. We seek to fill in gaps and try to avoid disjointed activities. Christ's promise to be present when two or three are gathered together in his Name (Mt 18:20) applies to more than prayer. Sharing with one another, God being present, produces a synergy or a geometric progression of ideas; choosing together among such ideas results in smoother, clearer, and more creative planning. Whether our colleagues are working at our side, or are the far-off writers of books to which we turn, we are never alone in the education task.

TO PLAN IS TO ASK A SEQUENCE OF QUESTIONS

The Setting

Who? Where? When? Who is there? Whom do we hope to include?
  Although "Education Is for Everyone," we must be aware of the needs of each specific group of learners.
Where will it be? What space is available? In what places can learning occur?
  Recognize all sorts of learning occasions (teenagers serving a parish supper, a Baptism, vestry planning time, stewardship programs).
  Comfortable space, lighting, decor help set the atmosphere but are secondary to the persons involved and to the message.
What time is most available? What time span is needed?
  Part of an hour? an evening? a weekend? Perhaps only a few minutes recurring daily? a series? 4, 6, 8, 13 weeks? a year-long event?
  A wide variety of time and space could be considered, but must be appropriate to the group and the topic.
  Examine and reexamine the situation.

The Leading Theme

About what main idea are we concerned?

Considering a common theme can give unity to a congregation's several programs. (Be sure the theme is inclusive enough and in context of the mission.)

A logical series of topics gives continuity.

The Church Year provides a framework of themes.

The Catechism in the BCP organizes the Outline of Faith into eighteen topics.

The Focus/Objectives

On what will we concentrate? What do we hope to accomplish?

Looking at an idea within a theme from several viewpoints, in a variety of ways, gives insights and understandings unexpectedly.

It is not necessary to teach all there is to know about a theme at one time. Search out the themes within themes within themes. Focus on one point; then, God willing, tomorrow and next year will bring more opportunities.

To avoid the frustration of an incomplete task, remember that the briefer the time available, the more pointed the focus must be.

Ways and Means

How will we learn? What are the alternatives? What are the resources available?

Consider alternative methods, since a wealth of ways and approaches can enrich learning.

"Resources" are people and places as well as books and activities.

Some ways of learning, arranged in order from least effective to most effective, are:

To Hear	"Teacher-Tell," lectures, sermons, reading aloud.
	(Being talked *with* greatly differs from being talked *at* or talked *to*.)
To See	Reading together, pictures, slides, graphs, objects.
To Identify With	Roles, skits, drama, field trips, creative writing.

To Have Firsthand Experience, Reflected Upon	We are challenged to be "doers of the Word and not hearers only" (Jas 1:22). And are told that "with knowledge and all discernment" we may "approve what is excellent and be pure and blameless for the day of Christ" (Phil 1:9–10).

To Combine All of the Above.

A change of pace stimulates imagination and avoids overworking any one sort of activity.

But remember to have a *reason* for every activity so it is pertinent to the focus and moves toward the objective. Both children and adults recognize purposeless busy-work.

Planning the Learning Event

Which activity will we choose? What are the learners going to *do?*

These questions cannot be the first answered, since decisions should be based upon answers in the preceding steps.

Also they should be activities which:

- actively involve most learners
- call for most creativity by learners
- contribute directly to the focus
- the leader has confidence in doing
- are appropriate to the age and skills of learners
- fit into time and space realistically

Remember that the one who is *doing* something is the one who is learning. What are the "students" going to do?

The Procedure

Who will do what? What is the schedule? Who has what responsibilities, before and during the event?

A format:

Orientation—Denote the beginning, clarify the purpose, give continuity.

Presentation—May be done by teacher or by others.

Exploration—Should always be done by the learners.

Creative Response—Should be encouraged by the learners.

Conclusion—May give carry-over, link to next occasion, or be a "cliff-hanger."

Being aware of about how long each activity should take helps avoid interruption or an unrealistic schedule.

The teacher needs to know what is the logical next step. Be prepared to move on to a parallel activity, or further exploration, or to summary reflection.

With a time scheme in mind, remain flexible to extend or cut short as responses call for. Knowing the focus will help avoid being side-tracked while still acknowledging concerns and interests of the group.

To backtrack or repeat simply for those who were absent previously denies the work of those who were present. If need be, include late-comers briefly by having learners review for them.

Responsibilities are best designated and shared as widely as possible by all persons involved.

The Evaluation

How will we know we have reached our objectives?

This is an essential question. We often treat review as an after-thought, casual and accidental. It should be intentional.

Reflection upon what has happened lets us see:

- how it fits in
- why it is important
- what it means to us
- what we are going to do about it.

Only then does learning truly become ours.

Knowledge is enhanced when learners can proceed to a next step and decide how to share it with someone else.

Preparing For the Next Advent

Where do we go next?

This leads us full circle, back to the first question.

Just as the Church Year is cyclical, each time Advent comes around we are different persons, changed by our experiences and relationships of the past twelve months, ready for new opportunities to grow in faith.

A QUESTION OF QUESTIONS

The role of the learner, as one on a quest, is to ask questions, and one of the teacher's responsibilities is to use questions carefully to stimulate and encourage the learner's reflection. The teacher must be a questioner as well, and certainly is in a position to accomplish the greatest learning. On the other hand, the role of the teacher *cannot* be that of someone with All the Answers. Many people are reluctant to volunteer as teachers because they feel they "don't know enough," when actually the chief requirement is a willingness to search, meanwhile enabling and organizing the journey that the whole group takes together as colearners.

THE TEACHER

The Teacher Is a Listener who is attentive enough to hear what the learners say; who is aware of what is unsaid; who responds without any judgment that would stifle; and who knows how to wait upon God.

The Teacher Is a Translator who puts the words of the Church into language that is understandable and images that are recognizable to the learners. "What is the meaning?" is the foremost question.

The Teacher Is a Custom Designer who tailors the curriculum for a specific moment to fit a specific group of learners—by awareness of their interests, skills, and experiences, and by planning and organizing their time together.

The Teacher Is a Pacesetter who provides a setting and an opportunity for learners to discover the Holy Spirit within a trusting and respecting community of explorers that cares for and accepts one another; who presents something to pique the learners' curiosity and stir up their questions.

QUESTIONS ARE USEFUL

For Information to recall specific facts, to seek data, or to determine what has been understood. The questions require correct answers, although the closed nature of such answers tends to limit discussion.

But too many such questions create a testing, competitive atmosphere where learners can be put on the defensive.

For Analysis to stimulate thinking further, to lead to conjectures, to dig for reasons, to evaluate a situation. These questions offer the possibility of several responses. Additional questions may follow naturally. ''Why . . .?'' and ''What do you think . . .?'' can initiate them.

But if thoughts are belittled, judged, or contradicted by others in group, open expression becomes reluctant or stifled.

For Personal Reactions to identify with, or to relate something to one's own life, as guides to discover values, to make decisions, to reflect. Answers will be interpretive, and might include ''What would you have done . . .?'', or ''When have you ever felt . . .?''

But it should be noted that many such questions do not contribute automatically to the learning of the whole group. To avoid invasion of privacy, reserve the learner's right to delay an answer or to be silent.

WAYS TO USE THIS GUIDE

The many components in the *Book of Common Prayer* are combined and offered in this volume to help you adapt and use them in your own setting so that each moment of learning can be unique. Although arranged in a timeline that moves through the Church Year, there is no one period in which any part must be learned. Christian education does not march in lockstep; it cannot race along with a stopwatch. Instead it lives in and responds to the recurring rhythms of the seasons. Everything will not happen at once. We will grow and learn more next year, from a different perspective, in God's good time.

Definition of the Season

Tells how the season is defined in time and in history.

Note the basic block of time the season spans.

Mark your calendar, to compare the Church dates with vacation calendars and national days which occur then, synchronizing it with scheduled events in your community and the world.

Note also the Fixed Holy Days and Lesser Feasts & Fasts to be commemorated during the season.

An interesting project can be research into how the season was observed early in history and how its meaning today has developed.

Themes

Describe the meaning of the season, and are taken from the scriptures and collects appointed to be read each Sunday (known as the Proper).

Choosing a theme gives a starting point for study.

In seasons with several related themes, one theme may be emphasized this year, another next.

Find out where in your community the theme of the season is being expressed today. Where can the theme be discovered in your daily paper? A bulletin board of clippings, a "journal," or a news broadcast could emphasize the theme in your parish.

Great Words

Offer a glance at different aspects of the themes of the season—the WORD and words.

Look for the story behind a word. (References such as *More Than Words* and *The Episcopalian's Dictionary* are helpful.)

Several words may be suggested to your group to build a litany or a poem.

Feature a "Word of the Week" in bulletin or poster or invent crossword puzzles or word games.

Ask "What experience have you had of (word)?" "Explain (word) as if to someone from another country, giving examples."

Choose a way to illustrate a word visually, with banners or dioramas or mobiles.

Through the Eyes of a Child

Begin the "translation" of theological themes for children using simple language and concepts.

Every leader, however, must remember the importance of clarity regardless of the student's age or level of sophistication and training.

Often children can understand visually or in actions what they cannot express in abstract words. Let them make their own pictures; let them act out ideas ad lib.

Ask yourself, "In terms of experiences known to these children, how can this idea be explained?"

Symbols and Traditions

A symbol stands for something else to which it is identified, and has meaning when the connection is recognized.

In any season symbols can be used in creative activities, and can be created from all sorts of materials.

In studying liturgies, identify the symbols and the symbolic actions for clues to learning.

Some traditions have long history, while others are recent in development. (See *The Book of Occasional Services*.) Local variations are infinite.

Traditions are preserved by being practiced. Look for the roots of traditions in your family and in your community.

Symbols help us learn about and understand neighbors of other cultures, and share in their seasonal traditions.

Social Justice Themes

Carry us beyond "Sundays only" into every day of our lives as Christians. They are drawn from the Proper for Sunday worship.

References are to general social issues, which could easily become specific and timely for a local educational event and/or an action group.

Issues can be the focus of debate or panel discussion.

Field trips offer closer involvement with an issue.

Such themes offer a challenge for Christians to consider whenever "mission" or "ministry" is studied.

Great Bible Stories

Are often found in the season's Lectionary and reflect its themes.

To study, read from more than one translation of the Bible. Referring to Bible Commentaries is helpful.

There is a variety of ways to retell a story: by paraphrasing, by showing slides or other illustrations, by redoing as a skit or other dramatization, or even by using puppets. Choose your own form of telling the story.

Choose one character in the reading with whom to identify. "What does it feel like to be that person?" "How would you act or respond?"

Asking questions can aid in reflecting on a Bible passage:

- What is the writer trying to say?
- What was the context or situation in which it was written?
- How is God speaking to us today and how does this passage reveal God's will to individuals and to the church?

Great Hymns

Are included as a reminder of the importance of hymnody in our worship and education.

The Hymnal is, in addition to the Bible and the BCP, the church's third major resource book for Christian education.

Children especially like repeated singing of familiar songs.

The words of hymns are significant for study, as expressions of the Church's faith.

The Episcopal Choirmaster's Handbook is an annual publication that offers more complete reference.

Canticles

Are songs or prayers, other than psalms, derived from the Bible (including the Apocrypha). This music of the ancient Church may be used similarly to hymns where appropriate in worship and for study.

The Book of Canticles provides further information and music.

Appropriate Services to Study

Are other than those usually held on Sundays (Holy Eucharist I & II, Morning Prayer I & II.) The suggestion of these services is intended to broaden familiarity with the richness of Anglican worship contained in *The Book of Common Prayer*.

Services can be read at home, or used for study. Discussion might seek analysis of form, historical usage, and significant personal impressions. Note how symbols and biblical images and ideas express the season's meaning.

Participation in corporate worship when possible is recommended along with study of the services. Liturgy is *doing*.

The Book of Occasional Services includes options in addition to those in *The Book of Common Prayer*.

Living the Season at Home and in the Parish

Suggests briefly a few activities suitable for diverse groups and occasions. This section offers ways of actively becoming involved in the themes of each season.

Further ideas can be found in the Suggested References and in many other current resources, such as *AWARE*.

The "Summary of the Lectionary" begins on page 90. For each Sunday in three-year cycle of psalms and lessons appointed for Sunday services, a brief summary of the readings is given. These are intended only as reminders of the subject. Reading the scriptures directly is important, followed by consulting a Bible commentary for additional clarity.

The themes of the Collects for each Sunday are summarized with the Lectionary.

"An Outline of the Faith commonly called the Catechism" (BCP page 845) is meant to be a summary for development by the teacher, providing a brief review of the Church's teaching. Each answer leads to the next question in an interwoven pattern of inquiry, but the arrangement under headings allows for selective use.

As an amplification of the sets of questions and answers in the Catechism, "An Index to the Outline of the Faith" on page 15 provides cross-references to seasonal information in this guide, and to scripture passages which are pertinent to each of the topics of the Faith.

It also may be used as a topical index to this guide.

SUGGESTED REFERENCES FOR USE WITH THE *GUIDE*

Liturgy and Worship

Advent to Pentecost, Buck, Morehouse-Barlow
The Book of Canticles, Church Hymnal Corporation
The Book of Occasional Services, Church Hymnal Corporation
Commentary on the American Prayer Book, Marion J. Hatchett, Seabury
The Episcopal Choirmaster's Handbook, Handbook Foundation, Sauk Center, Minn.
The Episcopalian's Dictionary, Howard Harper, Seabury
El Himnario Provisional, (in Spanish) permanent edition, called *El Himnario,* in preparation
The Hymnal, Church Hymnal Corporation
The Hymnal Companion, Church Hymnal Corporation
Hymns III, Church Hymnal Corporation
Keeping the Church Year, H. Boone Porter, Seabury
Lesser Feasts and Fasts, Church Hymnal Corporation
Lift Every Voice and Sing, Episcopal Commission for Black Ministries (available from Church Hymnal Corporation)
Liturgy For Living, Charles P. Price and Louis Weil, Seabury
Praying With the Family of God, Urban T. Holmes, Winston Press
Songs for Celebration, Church Hymnal Corporation

The Lectionary

Several translations of the Holy Bible
Introducing the Lessons of the Church Year, Frederick Borsch, Seabury
Sharing Our Biblical Story, Joseph P. Russell, Winston
Sunday's Scriptures, William Sydnor, Morehouse-Barlow

Learning Resources

Aware, Christian Education Resources, Executive Council of the Episcopal Church
Christian Education Catalogue, Ruth Gordon Cheney, ed., Seabury
Church School Teaching Can Be Fun, Schmelzel, Seabury
Classroom Creativity, Elizabeth Jeep, Seabury
Craft Handbook for Children's Church, Leslea Stringer & Lea Bowman, Baker Book House, Grand Rapids, Mich.
Equipping God's People, Gary T. Evans and Richard E. Hayes, Seabury
Teaching Teachers to Teach, Donald L. Griggs, Abingdon
The Whole Lay Ministry Catalogue, Barbara Kuhn, Seabury

AN INDEX TO THE OUTLINE OF THE FAITH

Topic:	Refer to Seasons:	Refer to Bible:
Human Nature (p. 845)	Advent Lent All Saints	Gen 1–3 Josh 22:16–19 Ps 107:11 Acts 7
God the Father (p. 846)	Easter Trinity Sunday	Gen 1:26–30 Lev 19:1–18 Ps 55:22 Col 1:16
The Old Covenant (pp. 846–47)	Advent	Gen 15 & 17 Ex 19:5; 34:27 Josh 24:25 2 Sam 23:5 Is 42:6 Mic 6:8
The Ten Commandments (pp. 847–48)	Lent Days after Pentecost	Ex 20:2–17 Deut 5:6–21 Rom 3:20ff
Sin and Redemption (pp. 848–49)	Advent Epiphany	Mt 16: 13–23 Mk 8:27–33

Topic:	Refer to Seasons:	Refer to Bible:
	Lent	Lk 9:18–22
	Holy Week	John 8:34–36
	All Saints	Rom 6:16–18
		1 John 2
God the Son (pp. 849–50)	Advent	Mt 1:18
	Christmas	Lk 1:35
	Epiphany	John 1:18
	Lent	Acts 2:24–30; 2:33
	Holy Week	Rom 8:16
	Easter	1 Cor 15:20ff
	Ascension	Phil 2:8
	Trinity Sunday	1 John 4:16
The New Covenant (pp. 850–51)	Advent	Jer 31:31
	Christmas	Mt 22:37; 28:19
	Easter	Mk 12:28
	Pentecost	Lk 10:25
	All Saints	John 10:10; 13:34
		Heb 8:7ff
The Creeds (pp. 851–52)	Epiphany	Mt 28:19
	Day of Pentecost	2 Cor 13:14
	Trinity Sunday	
	All Saints	
The Holy Spirit (pp. 852–53)	Easter	Gen 1:1
	Day of Pentecost	Is 42:1;59:21;61:1
	Trinity Sunday	Lk 4:18–19
	All Saints	John 14:7
		1 Cor 12:3
		2 Cor 3:17
		Eph 4:1–16
		2 Tim 3:16
The Holy Scriptures (pp. 853–54)	Advent	John 14:7
	Day of Pentecost	2 Tim 3:16
	Days after Pentecost	

Topic:	Refer to Seasons:	Refer to Bible:
The Church (pp. 854–55)	Day of Pentecost Days after Pentecost All Saints	Mt 28:16ff Rom 12 I Cor 12 Gal 6:16 Eph 1:22; 2:16; 2:22 Col 1:18 I Pet 2:9–10 I Tim 3:15
The Ministry (pp. 855–56)	Epiphany Day of Pentecost Days after Pentecost	Acts 7 & 15 I Pet 5:1ff Tit 1:7; 3:8 Heb
Prayer and Worship (pp. 856–57)	Advent Lent Easter Days after Pentecost	I Kings 18:29 & 36 Mt 6:9ff Lk 11:2ff; 24:53 Phil 4:6 I Tim 2:1 2 Tim 2:1 Jas 5:16 Rev 4
The Sacraments (pp. 857–58)	Epiphany Lent Holy Week All Saints	Mt 28:19 Rom 5:12–21 I Cor 11:23ff
Holy Baptism (pp. 858–59)	See BCP, p. 928 Epiphany Lent Easter Day of Pentecost All Saints	Mt 28:19
The Holy Eucharist (pp. 859–60)	Christmas Lent Holy Week	Mt 5:23–24; 26:17ff Mk 14:2ff Lk 22:7ff

Topic:	Refer to Seasons:	Refer to Bible:
	Easter	John 6:22–71
	Day of Pentecost	1 Cor 11:17–34
	All Saints	
Other Sacramental Rites (pp. 860–61)	Epiphany	Mt 19:3–6
	Lent	Mk 10:6–12
	Holy Week	John 20:22
	Easter	Acts 1:15–21; 6;
	Day of Pentecost	8:14–17; 19:17
	All Saints	Jas 5:13–14
The Christian Hope (pp. 861–62)	Advent	Mt 25:31
	Lent	John 1:6
	Easter	Rom 6:4; 8:39
	Trinity Sunday	1 Cor 15
	Days after Pentecost	1 Thess 4:13–17
	All Saints	2 Tim 4:1
		Rev 7:9–17; 21:5

Part I

OUTLINES OF THE SEASONS

The Advent Season

Definition

Advent means "coming" in Latin.

Advent is the first season of the Church Year. It has four Sundays; the first is the Sunday nearest November 30. The last day of Advent is always December 24.

Advent Themes

A Season of Preparation:

to prepare the Way of the Lord;

for the Messiah (Savior) promised by God and foretold by the Prophets;

for the expected coming of the baby Jesus, born of Mary at Bethlehem;

for Christ, the Prince of Peace, who is coming again at the close of this Age (called Eschaton) to rule as Lord over the promised Kingdom of God;

for each of us as we look at our own lives, ask God's forgiveness for our sins, and get ready, with God's help, to "live in harmony with God, within ourselves, with our neighbors, and with all creation" as we await and expect the coming Kingdom. (Catechism, BCP, 849)

Great Words of Advent

Angels (Messengers of God)
Annunciation
Anticipation
Apocalypse

Coming
Deliverance
Eschatology (End Time)
Expectation

Fulfillment	Messiah
Hope	Peace
Judgment	Preparation
Kingdom of God	Promise
Light of the World (vs. Darkness)	Prophet
Longing	Reconciliation
Maranatha—Come, Lord Jesus!	Redemption
(Rev 22:20)	Waiting

Advent Through the Eyes of a Child

In Advent, we the Church

> wait for the coming of the baby Jesus whom God gave to us and to all people because he loves us and has made all of us his family;

> celebrate God's promise to be with us now and always;

> remember that Jesus will come again in glory and loving power to make all things new. Then God's people will live together in love and peace;

> can understand Advent by experiences of waiting, hope, promises, and love in our lives now.

Advent Worship Sentence for Young Children

"Come down to dwell with us, Lord Jesus. Open our hearts to receive you."

Suggested hand motions: arms outstretched above head; hands brought down, arms crossed over heart on word "heart" and then opened wide at 45-degree angle.

Symbols and Traditions of Advent

Color—purple for preparation, penitence, and royalty.

Advent wreath—a green wreath with candles, one for each of the four Sundays.

Jesse Tree—a tree with symbols of Old Testament prophecies of Jesus' coming. Compare to your own family tree or one about your parish.

Empty creche—awaiting the Christ child.

Advent calendar—to count the days to Christmas.

Light contrasted with darkness—Jesus is the Light of the world.

The Gloria and other glorious hymns are omitted—as we solemnly prepare for Christ's coming.

The ''O'' Antiphons—study the hymn ''O Come, O come, Emmanuel'' with concordance and Bible.

A Solemn Procession with Carols—a traditional English Advent service.

The third Sunday of Advent, known as *Gaudete* (''Rejoice,'' from an ancient antiphon based on Philippians 4:4) *Sunday,* has an especially joyous emphasis, heightening the eager sense of anticipation as Advent moves toward its longed-for fulfillment. Like Refreshment Sunday in Lent, the joyful color rose may be used, and often the candle in the Advent wreath for this third Sunday will be rose or pink, instead of purple.

Local traditions—

Social Justice Themes for Advent

A time of Judgment as we look forward to the coming Kingdom and realize the sinfulness of the present age.

The Collects of the season give us a natural way of approaching ethical and social justice issues.

Advent 1

''. . . cast away the works of darkness,'' a phrase from Romans 13:11–14

- personal ethics—things we do as individuals that we are ashamed of when we hold those actions up in the light of Christ
- business ethics—looking at business practices that fail to measure up to the demands of the coming Kingdom

Advent 2

''. . . who sent your messengers the prophets to preach repentence and prepare the ways for our salvation''

The Advent Season 23

Social issues raised by Amos and Isaiah provide an outline of contemporary issues:

- corruption in public affairs
- oppression of peoples
- crushing and oppressing the poor by demanding a selfish, self-indulgent life style
- failing to carry out justice for the people
- practicing empty formalism in religion
- failing to be concerned for the good of the people
- relying on military power for security—the arms race
- failing to care for the poor, the widow, the orphan, and the disadvantaged
- forgetting the words of the Lord and concentrating on self-fulfillment in life
- seeking wealth by acquiring lands and acquisitions to the detriment of others (corporate ethical responsibility)
- a demand for freedom from want, from oppression, and from war (Isaiah 9:1–7)
- people who claim to speak the word of God but who instead mislead the people

Advent 4

". . . Jesus Christ, at his coming, may find in us a mansion prepared for himself"

- a demand that whatever we do personally and publicly will be done in a way that prepares the world for the coming of Christ in contrast to the rejection of Christ in biblical times

Great Bible Stories for Advent

The Prophecies in Isaiah:

- The Lord's sign to the House of David (Isaiah 7:13–14)
- Unto us a Son is given (Isaiah 9:6–7)
- The Stem of Jesse (Isaiah 11:1–5)
- The Peaceable Kingdom (Isaiah 11:6–9)
- Comfort ye, comfort ye, my people (Isaiah 40:1–8)

- He shall feed his flock like a shepherd (Isaiah 40:9–17)
- A light to the Gentiles (Isaiah 42:6–7)
- A man of sorrows (Isaiah 53)

Elizabeth:

- Mary visited her cousin (Luke 1:39–56)
- The birth of John the Baptist is promised (Luke 1:5–25)

John the Baptist:

- Jesus is baptized in the Jordan (Matthew 3:1–17), (Mark 1:9–11)
- Imprisonment and beheading (Matthew 14:1–12), (Mark 6:14–29)

Mary—The Annunciation: (Luke 1:26–56)

Joseph's Dream: (Matthew 1:18–25)

Great Hymns for Advent

Come, thou long-expected Jesus
O Come, O come, Emmanuel

ADVENT IN THE BOOK OF COMMON PRAYER

Opening Sentences of Scripture

Morning Prayer (BCP 37/75)

Antiphons

Morning Prayer (BCP 43/80)

Canticles

In keeping with Advent's contemplative mood, the Kyrie eleison or Trisagion is sung in place of the more joyful Gloria in excelsis.

The following may be sung as entrance songs, in place of the sequence, at the offertory, or during the communion of the people:

Canticle 9: The First Song of Isaiah (Ecce, Deus, BCP 86).

Canticle 3 or 15: The Song of Mary (Magnificat, BCP 50 or 91), especially on the Fourth Sunday of Advent.

Canticle 4 or 16: The Song of Zechariah (Benedictus Dominus Deus, BCP 50 or 92), especially on the Second and Third Sundays of Advent.

Canticle 11: The Third Song of Isaiah (Surge, illuminare, BCP 87).

Prefaces

Holy Eucharist (BCP 345/378)

Prayers and Thanksgivings

Eucharistic Prayer B (BCP 367–69)

Collects 6 and 7 (BCP 395), which conclude the Prayers of the People with Advent themes.

A Service with Advent Themes

Order of Worship for the Evening (BCP 108)

Living the Advent Season at Home and in the Parish

Make an Advent calendar (a really large one for the whole parish perhaps).

Start a collection of food, clothes, or toys in preparation for sharing Christmas love with someone who is needy.

Creative writing (a poem or story) on an Advent theme—hope or waiting or light, for example.

Mary was waiting . . . Luke 1:26–38. What is it that you are waiting for? Or discuss and share why hope is an Advent theme and what a message of hope might be for you.

Make an Advent Capsule (like a Time Capsule), to tell the children and adults of the parish twenty-five years from this Advent what is important to us today. Include news items that may be offered in a service with the Prayers of the People.

Make a "Promise Branch" using a real or paper tree branch tied with symbols of promises you mean to keep (a broom straw to sweep the floor, a pen to write a letter). Jesus is God's promised Messiah to us.

Express through visual arts (banners, bulletin boards, murals) some of the prophecies about the expected Messiah. How do they tell us and others what Jesus and the Kingdom of God are like?

Plan and keep an Advent discipline, perhaps daily Bible reading and reflection and shared prayer time.

Other local ideas

The Christmas Season

Definition

December 25 is the feast day on which we celebrate the birth of our Lord
Jesus Christ.

Our word *Christmas* comes from the old English "christmasse"
(Christ's Mass).

In ancient calendars it was set close to the winter solstice when the
sun returned light to the world.

Holy Days in the Christmas Season

December 26   St. Stephen, the first Christian martyr, stoned to death
(Acts 6:9–8:2) Symbols: stones and a palm branch

December 27   St. John, Apostle and Evangelist Symbol: an eagle

December 28   Holy Innocents—children killed by Herod at Bethlehem
(Matthew 2:16–18) Symbols: Crown with stars representing martyrdom.

January 1   The Holy Name of Our Lord Jesus Christ tells of the
naming of Jesus in accordance with divine plan. (Luke
2:21) *Jesus* means "the Lord saves," and in remembering his name we remember what God's love has done
for us.

Christmas Themes

Christ is born!

In the birth of Jesus, God gave us the greatest gift by becoming a
human being and dwelling among us. Jesus is truly God and truly human—the Incarnation is God's plan for reconciling and redeeming his
people.

In Christ we, who are made in the image of God, behold the dignity of our human nature without sin. Because Christ came to save us, we have hope and assurance of sharing his life both now and always.

Great Words of Christmas

Angels	Nativity
Annunciation	New light
Celebration	Outreach
Fulfillment	Reconciliation
Incarnation	Redeemer
Judge	Savior

Christmas Through the Eyes of a Child

At Christmas, we the Church

welcome our Lord Jesus Christ and joyfully celebrate his birthday;

thank God for his greatest gift of love to us, his Son, Jesus Christ;

Christmas Worship Sentence for Young Children

"Rejoice, rejoice!
God has come to be a child like us.
Rejoice, rejoice!"

Arms are raised from the side of the body, crossing arms and sweeping them open again and holding them outstretched. Repeat. Arms brought down, hands touch chest. Rejoice motion repeated twice.

Symbols and Traditions of Christmas

Color—white for festival and joy
    Angels—they rejoiced at Jesus' birth
    Candles—Jesus is the Light of the world
    Chrismons—symbols about Jesus as tree ornaments
    Crèche (manger scene)
    Evergreen garlands and wreaths (holly, laurel, mistletoe) for everlasting life

Gifts—to share and show love as God has done
St. Nicholas/Santa Claus
Sheep and shepherds
Star
A Festival of Lessons and Carols—a traditional English Christmas service
Local traditions—

Great Bible Stories for Christmas

The birth and childhood of Jesus (Luke 2:1–40)
  The flight into Egypt (Matthew 2:1–15)

Great Hymns of Christmas

Break forth, O beauteous heavenly light
What child is this
*All glory be to God on high (metrical setting of the Gloria in excelsis)

CHRISTMAS IN THE BOOK OF COMMON PRAYER

Opening Sentences of Scripture
Morning Prayer (BCP 37/75)

Antiphons
Morning Prayer (BCP 43/80)

Canticles
Canticle 6 or 20: The Song of the Angels (Gloria in excelsis, BCP 52/94)
  Canticle 3 or 15: The Song of Mary (Magnificat, BCP 50/91)

Prefaces
Holy Eucharist (BCP 345/378; note that this Preface is designated for the Incarnation. It is also used on the Feast of St. Mary the Virgin on August 15.)

Prayers and Thanksgivings
Eucharistic Prayer B (BCP 367–69)

Living the Christmas Season at Home and in the Parish

Families and parishes develop their own traditions for celebrating Jesus' birthday. These often include gifts for others, such as clothing, toys, food, or money for persons in need. These gifts should be expressions of the love of Christ, not one-time Christmas projects.

Small trimmed Christmas trees can be made and shared with people who are ill or homebound.

The *posada* (meaning "inn" in Spanish) is a tradition of Mexico and other Latin American countries which can be observed or adapted. A procession with figures of Mary and Joseph goes from house to house (or room to room or in Church) looking for a place of shelter. Sometimes the procession begins nine days before Christmas, which can give it an Advent flavor of expectation, but always whenever the "inn" is reached, the innkeeper, after asking a series of questions, lets them enter. (Questions include "Who is knocking?; Where have you come from?; What do you want here?") The figures are brought to the manger. If it is Christmas Eve, the figure of the Christ Child is added, and a celebration with singing and dancing and feasting may follow. The *posada* dramatizes acceptance of the Christ Child in our lives and hearts.

Candles can be made especially to burn during the Christmas season, perhaps every night until Twelfth Night. Doorways and walks can be lined with *luminarias,* according to a custom begun first in the old southwestern United States. These candles, placed on a bed of sand inside brown paper bags, give off an amber glow. Fold down the top of an ordinary No. 8 or 10 grocery bag about two inches to make it stay open. Place a household candle firmly into the two-inch bed of sand at the bottom of the bag. Lighted at dusk and placed two or three feet apart along lawns or steps, the candles will burn gently for several hours and snuff out when they burn down to the sand base.

Make a Christingle—an orange decorated with a lighted candle, raisins, and nuts. The orange represents the world, a red ribbon tied around the equator is the Blood of Christ, and the raisins and nuts are the fruits of the earth. The candle is the Light of the World. Christingles (a Moravian custom) might be shared as gifts or lighted from the Christ candle at church or at home. They could be lighted at the end of a service and carried, symbolically, out into the world.

Other local ideas

The Epiphany Season

Definition
The Epiphany or Manifestation of Christ to the Gentiles is observed on January 6.

Epiphany comes from a Greek word meaning "showing forth," "appearance," "manifestation," "revelation." Jesus is the manifestation of God.

The Eve of the Feast of the Epiphany (Twelfth Night) marks the end of the Christmas Season. The Epiphany Season is variable in length. It depends upon the date of Easter and may include as many as nine Sundays or as few as four.

Holy Days in Epiphany
January 18 Confession of St. Peter (BCP 187/238)
January 25 Conversion of St. Paul (BCP 187/238)
February 2 Presentation of Jesus in the Temple (BCP 187/239)

Epiphany Themes
Manifestation of Christ to the whole world. When we see Christ we are seeing God.

Epiphany is a time for remembering the recognition of Jesus as God by many people, among them the magi, John the Baptist, Jesus' disciples, and by those who have been Christians in every age, including our own.

Epiphany is a time for rededicating ourselves to our own ministries and our missionary task—to continue the spread of Jesus' light in the world.

In Epiphany we remember Christ's baptism and our own. Just as the disciples were called, we received our calling or vocation as Christians through our baptism.

The Sacraments are a manifestation of Christ to the Church.

Epiphany is a time for remembering the signs of Jesus that showed him forth to the people as in the first miracle at Cana and in the healing miracles. Healing and the anointing of the sick are important themes of this season.

Great Words of Epiphany

Apostle	Miracle
Baptism	Mission
Calling	Outreach
Conversion	Revelation
Covenant	Shining star
Disciple	Showing forth
Gifts and treasures	Sign
Light	Wise men (magi)
Ministry	

Epiphany Through the Eyes of a Child

What Jesus did and said helps us to know who God is and what he is doing for us:

Jesus called his friends to be with him and to help him in his work;
Jesus came for all the people of the world;
Jesus is like a light, helping us to see better;
We are baptized into God's family, the Church.

Epiphany Worship Sentence for Young Children

"You show us your love in the Light
that shines in the darkness."

Hands above head outstretched at 60-degree angle, arms brought to cross on chest, then raise arms above head. Arms continue down to 180-degree angle.

Symbols and Traditions of Epiphany

Color—white, the festival color, for the Feast of the Epiphany and the days up to and including the next Sunday, which is the Feast of Our Lord's Baptism.

Green for the rest of the season, the color of the ongoing life of the Church.

The Feast of Lights emphasizes the theme of the Light of the World, the True Light. Candlelight services are often held in cathedrals and parish churches on the Feast of the Epiphany or on any succeeding Sunday in the Season.

Witness and participation in baptism, especially on the Feast of Jesus' Baptism, the First Sunday after the Epiphany.

The Wise Men—Magi—Three Kings   Matthew's gospel (Matthew 2:1–12) tells of wise men (people who studied the movement of the stars to interpret their meaning) who came from the east, following a special star and bringing gifts to the child Jesus. They were Gentiles, not Jews, and they worshipped him. The story of the Wise Men that we know is grounded in legends that came out of the Middle Ages. The men were described as kings, and we often hear their names as Melchior, Caspar, and Balthazar.

The Gifts of the Wise Men (as described in Matthew):

Gold for royalty, wealth, the Kingship of Christ.

Frankincense, made from gum from an Asian and African tree. It may be burned to produce aromatic smoke used in worship; it symbolizes divinity and prayer.

Myrrh, a bitter resin used by people in ancient times to anoint bodies before burial; a symbol of suffering and death, foretelling Christ's giving of self and death.

A single *Star* to recall the manifestation of Christ to the world in the revelation to the Wise Men.

Candlemas (Candle Mass), February 2, takes its name from the candles carried at the celebration of the Presentation of Christ in the Temple (see *The Book of Occasional Services,* p. 51). It celebrates a ritual of Jewish law related to first-born sons which Joseph and Mary carried out also (Luke 2:21–40). Luke's gospel tells how Simeon and Anna, devout Jews, honored the infant Jesus as the promised Messiah.

Local traditions—

Social Justice Themes for Epiphany

Epiphany 1

Baptism of our Lord

"Grant that all who are baptized into his name may keep the covenant they have made . . ."

The Baptismal Covenant calls Christians to strive for justice and peace among all people, and respect the dignity of every human being. (BCP 304)

Epiphany 6

". . . in keeping your commandments . . ."

Six of the ten commandments remind us that to honor God is to love others as we love ourselves. The Ten Commandments summarize the 613 commandments of the Torah. Many of these commandments deal with proper treatment of the poor, the stranger, the disadvantaged in society. They demand ethical business practices.

Jesus' "new Law" outlined in the Sermon on the Mount calls the Christian to an even higher standard of justice. Specifically:

- reconciliation—at the root of killing is anger; the Christian must work for peace
- human sexuality
- marital relationships
- dealing truthfully in business, personal, and political matters
- demand for extraordinary justice
- human rights
- love for all people, even those perceived to be enemies, an impelling call to work for peace

Great Bible Stories for Epiphany

Moses and the Burning Bush (Exodus 3:1–10)
Visit of the Magi (Matthew 2:1–3, 9–11)

The Epiphany Season 35

Presentation of Jesus in the Temple (Luke 2:22–39)
The Marriage in Cana (John 2:1–11)
Calling of the Disciples:

- The first disciples (Matthew 4:18–22; Mark 1:16–20; Luke 5:1–11; John 1:35–51; 21:1–8)
- Names of the Twelve (Matthew 10:1–4; Mark 3:3–19; Luke 6:12–16)
- Matthew called (Matthew 9:9–13; Mark 2:13–17; Luke 5:27–35)
- Philip called (John 1:43–51)

Some Healing Miracles:
- The daughter of the Canaanite woman (Matthew 15:21–28)
- The epileptic boy (Matthew 17:14–18)
- The two blind men (Matthew 20:29–34)
- A leper healed (Matthew 8:1–4; Mark 1:40–45)
- The centurion's servant (Matthew 8:5–10; Luke 7:1–10)
- The paralytic (Matthew 9:1–8; Mark 2:1–12; Luke 5:17–26)
- The demoniac (Matthew 17:1–8; Mark 5:1–20; Luke 8:26–39)

The Transfiguration (Matthew 17:1–8; Mark 9:1–8; Luke 8:28–36)
Conversion of St. Paul (Acts 9)

Great Hymns of Epiphany

We three kings of Orient are
What star is this, with beams so bright

Some Special Dates in Epiphany

January 15   Birthday of Martin Luther King
February 4   Cornelius the Centurion
February 13   Absalom Jones, Priest

EPIPHANY IN THE BOOK OF COMMON PRAYER

Opening Sentences of Scripture

Morning Prayer (BCP 38/76)

36   Outline of the Seasons

Antiphons

Morning Prayer (BCP 43/81)

Canticles

Canticle 9: The First Song of Isaiah (Ecce, Deus, BCP 86)
Canticle 10: The Second Song of Isaiah (Quaerite Dominum, BCP 86)
Canticle 11: The Third Song of Isaiah (Surge, illuminare, BCP 87)
Canticle 4 or 16: The Song of Zechariah (Benedictus Dominus Deus, BCP 50, 92)
Canticle 5 or 17: The Song of Simeon (Nunc dimittis, BCP 51, 93)
(Especially appropriate on the Feast of the Presentation of Christ in the Temple and during the last part of the Epiphany Season. Because of the text of the first verse, some may find this canticle more appropriately sung following a reading than as a hymn of praise in the first part of the Eucharist.)

Prefaces

Holy Eucharist (BCP 346/378)

Prayers and Thanksgivings

Eucharistic Prayer B (BCP 367–69)
Thanksgiving for the Mission of the Church (BCP 838)
Collect for the Mission of the Church (BCP 206/257)
Thanksgiving for the Restoration of Health (BCP 841)
Collect: Of a Missionary (BCP 196/247)
Thanksgiving for the Gift of a Child (BCP 841)

Services with Epiphany Themes

Service of Ministration to the Sick (BCP 453)
Holy Baptism (BCP 299)
Confirmation (BCP 413)
A Form of Commitment to Christian Service (BCP 420)
Ordination (Bishop, Priest, Deacon) (BCP 511–55)
Celebration of a New Ministry (BCP 559)
An Order of Worship for the Evening (BCP 108)

Living the Epiphany Season at Home and in the Parish

Baptism—sign of God's people
   Particularly be aware of baptisms in this season. Suggest that children ask their parents about their own baptisms. Make gifts for the persons to be baptized (such as a baptismal candle). Discuss and plan ways that everyone in the faith community can support the newly baptized.

Procession of the Kings
   Have a procession of the three Kings, robed and bearing their gifts to the crèche as part of the liturgy on the Feast of the Epiphany.

An Epiphany Celebration
   A parish party could include an Epiphany cake, caroling, and a visit from the three Kings who might distribute gifts, especially to the children. The Magi are an important emphasis among many Latin American and Spanish-speaking groups. In Spain, Costa Rica, and Puerto Rico children fill their shoes with straw for the Magi's camels, later finding presents in their place given by the Kings, a reminder of the gifts to the Christ Child.

Healing in your community
   Arrange visits with persons in the healing professions. How can you help them?

Celebration of Gifts
   Epiphany's theme of gifts makes it a time to remember and think about our own talents and gifts of the Spirit for mission and ministry, celebrating them and asking God to help us develop and offer them for others.

Other local ideas

The Lenten Season

Definition

From the Anglo-Saxon word "lencten"—the time of year when the days grow long.

The season begins on Ash Wednesday and ends on the Saturday before Easter (Holy Saturday), covering 40 days (excluding Sundays).

Since every Sunday is a "little Easter" celebrating the Resurrection, Sundays remain as feast days, even during the solemn Lenten Season.

Five Lenten Sundays are followed by the Sunday of the Passion, Palm Sunday, which begins Holy Week, when we relive the events of Jesus Christ's suffering and death.

In the early Church, Lent was the time of preparation for Easter baptism of converts to the Faith. Persons who were to receive the sacrament of baptism—"new birth," "death to sin"—were expected to fast and prepare for baptism.

Holy Days in Lent

Because Lent is determined by the movable date of Easter Day, it is necessary to check the Calendar of the Church Year (BCP 15–33) for Holy Days, Lesser Feasts, or other special observances which occur in a particular year.

Lenten Themes

Honest examination and repentance of our sins, and the renewal and strengthening of our spiritual lives both personally and within the community of the Church.

A time of reflection and contemplation, especially about salvation from bondage, as in the events of the Exodus and in our redemption from the bondage of our sins.

Fasting—the forty weekdays of Lent represent the days of fasting and temptation that Jesus spent in the wilderness. Experiences of self-denial are opportunities of discipline and the sacrifice of our will to the purpose of God.

A time for reconciliation with others.

The nature of the ministry of Jesus and what it means to be a disciple.

Great Words of the Lenten Season

Atonement
Calvary
Catechesis (teaching
  of the Faith)
Contrition
Cross
Crucifix
Fasting
Humility
Meditation
Overcoming temptation
Penitence

Pilgrimage
Preparation
Redemption
Return to God
Sacrifice
Salvation
Self-denial
Social justice
Reconciliation
Wilderness

Lent Through the Eyes of a Child

Lent is

a time for looking at the things we do that are wrong or that tempt us, asking God's and other people's forgiveness;

a time for giving up things that keep us from being loving people;

a time for doing extra things that will help us grow closer to God;

a time to be more aware of what it means to love as God loves us;

a time to ask God to help us to be more loving, remembering that God is always ready to strengthen us.

Lenten Worship Sentence for Young Children

"Lent is a time to prepare for Easter. Let us get ready for new life!"

Both hands make the sign of the cross, then a quick raising of the arms straight up. (Alternative: Arms are folded on chest, and body is slightly bowed at the waist. Then the quick arm sweep, ending with arms above head.)

Symbols and Traditions of Lent

Color—purple, for penitence and royalty; or the Lenten Array: cream, tan, or white—unbleached, raw, plain, and austere, to reflect the mood of Lent (based upon the sackcloth of Old Testament mourning).

Ashes—prepared from the previous year's palms for Ash Wednesday to symbolize our mortality and sorrow for our sins. The people of the Old Testament put ashes on their foreheads as a sign of penitence. Job (Job 42:6) and the King of Nineveh (Jonah 3:6) repented in ashes, wearing sackcloth.

Omitted from worship are Alleluias, joyful canticles, the Gloria in excelsis; these are replaced by songs and responses which are more in keeping with Lent's contemplative mood.

Vestments and hangings are more austere and solemn; flowers may be omitted from the altar.

Shrove Tuesday—On this day before Lent begins it was the custom to use up all milk, eggs, and fat in a household since these were not allowed in the strict fasting of Lent. The ingredients were made into pancakes, a meal which came to symbolize preparation for the discipline of Lent. Shrovetide, the three days of which Tuesday marks the end, comes from the verb "to shrive" (confess), referring to the ancient practice of confessing sins and receiving absolution in order to begin and keep a holy Lent.

The Cross—symbol of Christ and his sacrifice, love, salvation, redemption, atonement, and victory.

Time set aside for

teaching and learning

spiritual growth

fasting and self-denial

meditation and retreats.

Stations of the Cross—began when the Holy Land was in the hands of

Muslims. Wooden crosses with plaques, depicting the events of Jesus' route to Calvary, provided opportunity for devotions along the *Via Dolorosa* (Way of Sorrow).

Refreshment Sunday (also Mid-Lent Sunday)—the fourth Sunday in Lent when the Gospel speaks of Jesus feeding the five thousand, and Lenten discipline was relaxed to remind Christians of the true Bread, Jesus, who gives life to the world. The English often interrupted the Lenten fast with simnel cakes, a traditional and very rich sweet.

Mothering Sunday—In England children away from home at school or work were permitted to go home to visit their mothers and/or to visit their cathedral or mother church on this fourth Sunday in Lent.

Preparation for Baptism—historically and still a period to prepare for the baptisms and confirmations that occur traditionally at the Vigil of Easter Eve.

Local traditions—

Social Justice Themes for Lent

Ash Wednesday

Ethical issues raised in the Litany for Penitence

- exploitation of peoples to satisfy our self-indulgent appetites
- dishonesty in daily life and work
- blindness to human need and suffering—world hunger
- indifference to injustice and cruelty
- prejudice and contempt towards those who differ from us
- waste and pollution of God's creation

Second Sunday in Lent

God's mercy for us calls for mercy from us

- criminal justice issues
- death penalty
- treatment of refugees and displaced persons coming into our nation

Great Bible Stories for Lent

The Story of the Creation and Fall (Genesis, Chapters 2–3)
The Flood—God's Promise to Noah (Genesis, Chapters 6–9)

God's Call to Abraham (Genesis 12:1–8)
Abraham's Test With His Son Isaac (Genesis 22:1–19)
The Joseph Story (Genesis, Chapters 30–50)
David and Bathsheba (II Samuel, Chapter 11)
The Story of Jonah (Jonah, Chapters 1–4)
The Temptations of Jesus (Matthew 4:1–11, Mark 1:12–13, Luke 4:1–13)
Parable of the Prodigal Son (Luke 15:11–32)
Zacchaeus (Luke 19:1–10)
Feeding of the Five Thousand (John 6:4–15)

Great Hymns of Lent

Forty days and forty nights
The glory of these forty days

THE LENTEN SEASON IN THE BOOK OF COMMON PRAYER

Opening Sentences of Scripture

Morning Prayer (BCP 38/76)

Antiphons

Morning Prayer (BCP 43/81)

Canticles

Kyrie eleison or Trisagion is sung in place of the Gloria in excelsis at the Eucharist.

The following may be sung as entrance songs, in place of the sequence, at the offertory, or during the communion of the people:

Canticle 14 (BCP 90): A Song of Penitence (Kyrie Pantokrator)

Canticle 10 (BCP 86): The Second Song of Isaiah (Quaerite Dominum)

Prefaces

Holy Eucharist (BCP 346/379)

The Lenten Season   *43*

Prayers and Thanksgivings

Eucharistic Prayer A (BCP 361–63)
Eucharistic Prayer C (BCP 369–72)

Services with Lenten Themes

The Daily Office (BCP 37–143)
Reconciliation of a Penitent (BCP 447)
A Penitential Order: Rite One (BCP 319)
A Penitential Order: Rite Two (BCP 351)
The Great Litany (BCP 148)
Burial of the Dead: Rite One (BCP 469)
Burial of the Dead: Rite Two (BCP 491)
Ministration at the Time of Death (BCP 462)
The Holy Eucharist: Rite One (BCP 323)
The Holy Eucharist: Rite Two (BCP 355)

Living the Lenten Season at Home and in the Parish

Writing and illustrating Litanies of Penitence by children and/or adults.

Dramatization of Gospel lessons and other readings which are especially rich in Lent and lend themselves to participation by a large group. Think about using taped "radio plays" or sound effects, or about using slides or pantomime or puppets or shadow plays, as well as choral reading and more usual dramatic presentations.

A Study or review of our faith as Episcopalians might focus upon the Outline of the Faith (BCP 843–62).

Bury the Alleluia—a medieval Christian tradition. Make an "Alleluia" as a painting, small banner, plaque (possibilities are numerous), wrap it in plastic to protect it, put it in a box and bury it on the last Sunday *before* Lent. On Easter Day dig it up and display it, singing, "Jesus Christ is risen today! Alleluia!"

Jesus the True Bread is part of the collect of Lent's fourth Sunday. A day for family bread baking, or baking bread for a Eucharist (perhaps for Easter Day). Fancy breads can be frozen for an Easter feast.

A Lenten Pilgrimage can offer opportunities for reading and reflection done either in one time span or for a certain amount of time each week. It can be done at home or at designated spots in the church building when there can be periods of solitude and quiet. Instructions may include bringing a Bible, paper, and pencil, and a simple guidesheet will help the "pilgrim" begin. Brief suggested readings might be the Epistles or other readings for Lent, one for each "station," with a short commentary and questions to aid in reflection. "Pilgrims" move at their own pace, using the guidesheet to meet their own schedule and needs. Perhaps the last "station" will be the altar rail, reading an account of the Easter story or some other passage that points toward the climax for which Lent is a preparation.

Remembering our heritage, some selections that might be memorized are:

- The Lord's Prayer (BCP 97)
- The Apostles' Creed (BCP 53/96)
- The Ten Commandments (BCP 317/350)
- The names of the Books of the New Testament
- The Twenty-third Psalm
  (The familiar King James version may be found in the Burial Office, Rite One, BCP 476)
- A Table Blessing (BCP 835)
- A Collect for the Renewal of Life (BCP 99)
- Antiphon of the Song of Simeon (BCP 134)
  "Guide us waking, O Lord," etc.
- A Prayer: "Keep watch, dear Lord, with those who work" etc. (BCP 134)

Other local ideas

Holy Week

Definition

A week in which we as the Church dramatize the events which led up to and include the suffering and death of Jesus on the Cross.

Holy Week begins with the Sunday of the Passion, or Palm Sunday, and the joyous triumphal entry into Jerusalem, and ends with the sombreness of crucifixion and death.

The name of Maundy Thursday comes from the Latin *mandatum* or "command," from the two commands which Jesus gave his disciples at the Last Supper: to celebrate the Eucharist and to love and serve one another as he had loved and served them.

Good Friday commemorates the crucifixion of Our Lord. It is known as "Good" because of the new life brought about by His victory of the Cross.

Holy Week Themes

The theme of Holy Week is one of Passion, the ultimate in love and caring. John's gospel gives us Jesus' definition of Passion: "Greater love has no man than this, that a man lay down his life for his friends." (John.15:13) Jesus gives his life to save our lives from sin and death. Because of our self-centeredness, we are unable to save ourselves. He *atones* for our sin.

It is because we share Christ's victory over sin and death that we face the Cross feeling sadness and remorse but also deeply thankful for what we have been given. Good Friday is about triumph.

The tension between suffering and glorious triumph is set immediately before us on Palm Sunday, when joyful hosannas ring out even as the sense of foreboding grows. Jesus enters Jerusalem proclaimed as a king, riding toward a destiny of suffering and death amid the shouts of those who soon will turn against him.

Maundy Thursday recalls the Last Supper when Jesus commanded his disciples and us to do two things—the two things he did in the Upper Room. He broke bread with them, saying, "Do this for the remembrance of me." In the Eucharist we have the promise of his presence with us always. When he washed the disciples' feet, he commanded them to follow his example to love and humbly serve one another.

Holy Saturday is a time for reflecting upon Jesus' death and burial and what it means for our lives. It is the calm after the storm as we await the sunrise.

Great Words of Holy Week

Atonement	Hosanna
Broken Bread	Holy Mysteries
Calvary	Humility
Christus Victor	Lash
Crown of Thorns	Last Supper
Crucifix	Passion
Crucifixion	Redemption
Cup of Wine	Remembrance
Denial of Peter	Suffering
Foot Washing	Tomb (Sepulcher)
Gethsemane	Trail before Pilate
Golgotha	Walking in the Way of the Cross
	The Watch

Holy Week Through the Eyes of a Child

When Jesus rode into Jerusalem on the back of a donkey, the people who greeted him expected a powerful hero. They did not understand that Jesus' power was not physical strength, but loving and caring.

Jesus showed us that we are to remember him and follow his example of caring for and serving others. We remember him in the Eucharist when we know he is present with us. We see his example of humbly serving others in love in his washing of the disciples' feet.

Jesus proclaimed God's forgiveness from the Cross in spite of what happened in Holy Week. He forgave Peter who denied him, and those who caused his death, and he will forgive us. That's why Good Friday is *good*.

As God was with Jesus in his suffering and dying, he is with us when we suffer.

Symbols and Traditions of Holy Week

Color—red (crimson); or purple as in Lent.

Palms—fronds for the Procession on Palm Sunday. The people in Jerusalem waved them joyously as we might wave flags in a parade.

Donkey—the "colt of an ass" on which Jesus rode into Jerusalem; symbol of humility.

Veiling the cross—sometimes done throughout Holy Week; it is unveiled at Easter to reveal the empty cross of resurrection. A plain wooden cross is used on Good Friday.

Bowl and Towel—reminders of Jesus' act of washing the disciples' feet; symbols of service and humility.

Blessing of oils—the Bishop may bless holy oils to be used throughout the year at a special Eucharist in Holy Week.

Rooster—reminder of Peter's denial of Jesus before the cock crowed.

Silencing of the organ—some parishes silence the organ from the Maundy Thursday Liturgy until the Gloria at the Easter Vigil.

Traditionally the altar is stripped (and washed) after the Eucharist on Maundy Thursday. No hangings remain until the Easter Vigil.

Crown of Thorns—a Good Friday symbol (from Matthew 27:29 and John 19:2) because the soldiers mocked Jesus as a king, dressing him in a purple robe and placing a crown of thorns on his head.

Crucifix—cross with the image of the crucified Jesus upon it. A Good Friday symbol of suffering.

Dogwood—according to legend, the dogwood with its cross-shaped blossom, marked as though there were nail prints in it, may have been used to build the cross.

Lamb—Jesus, called the Lamb of God, was sacrificed like a Passover Lamb. "Christ our Passover is sacrificed for us." (BCP 364)

Sand dollar—a legendary symbol of Good Friday because of the five wounds of Jesus which appear to be depicted: four nail marks and the mark of the soldier's spear. (John 19:34)

When Holy Communion is administered on Good Friday it is from the reserved sacrament, that is, from bread and wine consecrated at a previous Eucharist and reverently kept for a future communion. The elements reserved for Good Friday are consecrated at the Maundy Thursday

Eucharist because it is the commemoration of Jesus' Last Supper with his disciples. Reserving the bread and wine reminds us of this occasion when the Eucharist was instituted and reminds us of the sacrificial aspect of communion on Good Friday, the day of Jesus' sacrifice on the Cross. In bread and wine we remember that Jesus' body was broken and his blood was shed—for us and for the world.

Holy Saturday, as noted in the rubric for that day, is the only day in the Church Year on which there is no communion, only a Liturgy of the Word (BCP 283) to ponder as we await the third day.

Local traditions—

Social Justice Themes for Holy Week

Palm Sunday

"...mercifully grant that we may walk in the way of his suffering..." (Collect, BCP 272)

- a call to identify with the suffering peoples of the nation and the world and not remain aloof
- compassion for God's people everywhere, for "all sorts and conditions" of people (BCP 814)

Great Bible Stories for Holy Week

The Anointing at Bethany: Matthew 26:6–13, Mark 14:3–9, John 12:1–8
Triumphal Entry into Jerusalem: Matthew 21:1–9, Mark 11:1–10, Luke 19:28–38, John 12:12–19
Cleansing of the Temple: Mark 11:15–19, Luke 19:47–48
Conspiracy against Jesus: Matthew 26:1–5, Mark 14:1–2, Luke 22:1–2, John 11:45–47
Betrayal by Judas: Matthew 26:14–16, 20–25; Mark 14:10–11, 17–22; Luke 22:3–6,14; John 13:1–2, 18–30
The Footwashing: John 13:3–17, 34–35
Lord's Supper: Matthew 26:26–29; Mark 14:22–25; Luke 22:21–38; John 7:41–59
Peter's Denial: Matthew 26:30–35, 57–75; Mark 14:26–31, 53–72; Luke 22:31–34, 39, 54–71; John 13:36–38, 18:15–18, 25–27
Jesus in Gethsemane: Matthew 26:30–35; Mark 14:32–42; Luke 22:40–46; John 18:1

Jesus taken Prisoner: Matthew 26:47–56; Mark 14:43–52; Luke 22:47–53; John 18:2–12

Jesus on Trial: Matthew 26:57–75, 27:1–2,11–14; Mark 14:53–72, 15:1–5; Luke 22:54–71, 23:2–5; John 18:13–14, 19–24, 28, 19:1–15

Jesus before Herod: Luke 23:6–16

Jesus Sentenced to Die: Matthew 27:15–26; Mark 15:6–15; Luke 23:17–25; John 28:16

Jesus Mocked: Matthew 27:27–31; Mark 15:16–20; John 19:1–3

The Road to Golgotha: Matthew 27:32; Mark 15:21; Luke 23:26–32; John 19:17

Crucifixion and Death: Matthew 27:33–56; Mark 15:22–41; Luke 23:33–49; John 19:17–30

Jesus' Burial: Matthew 27:57–61; Mark 15:42–47; Luke 23:50–56; John 19:31–42

Guard at the Tomb: Matthew 27:62–66

Great Hymns of Holy Week

Palm Sunday	All glory, laud, and honor
Maundy Thursday	Now my tongue, the mystery telling
Good Friday	Where charity and love prevail (*Ubi caritas*)
	Alone thou goest forth, O Lord
	Sing, my tongue, the glorious battle

HOLY WEEK IN THE BOOK OF COMMON PRAYER

Opening Sentences of Scripture

Morning Prayer (BCP 39/76)

Prefaces

Holy Eucharist (BCP 346/379)

Prayers and Thanksgivings

Eucharistic Prayer—Rite I (BCP 334–36)
Eucharistic Prayer A (BCP 362–63)
Eucharistic Prayer C (BCP 369–72)

Benedictus qui venit is about the Palm Sunday event of Our Lord's triumphal entry in Jerusalem (Matthew 21:9). It is found on BCP pages 334, 341, 362, 367, 371, and 373.

A Collect for Fridays remembers the victory of Good Friday on every Friday (BCP 56, 69, 99, 123).

A Collect for Noonday remembers the crucifixion which took place at this hour (BCP 107).

The Collect "Of the Holy Cross" is on BCP 201/252.

Services with Holy Week Themes

Proper Liturgies for Holy Week:
Palm Sunday BCP 270
Maundy Thursday BCP 274
Good Friday BCP 276
Holy Saturday BCP 283

Living Holy Week at Home and in the Parish

Making dioramas or arranging several rooms as scenes from the main events of Holy Week can clarify our understanding of the happenings which they portray. A guided tour or narration can explain the scenes to visitors.

A crown of thorns can be made by soaking stems of a plant with thorns until they are pliable enough to shape. Wire or tie together to hold the shape as the stems dry out. Use the symbol in worship or in a place of meditation.

Make a large wooden cross, to be used as the rubric for the Good Friday liturgy (BCP 281) indicates.

A tape recording could give the details of Jesus' way to Calvary as a radio or television reporter might describe them.

Make a list of every adjective you can think of that describes the feelings of those who were there and yours about Holy Week. Or use colors to express these feelings.

Using gestures in silence act out a Holy Week hymn, such as "Alone thou goest forth, O Lord."

Bend large nails to make a small cross for Holy Week devotions.

Study the various kinds of crosses throughout Christian history to make examples for display.

Other local ideas

The Easter Season

Definition

Easter is a festival season whose first day is Easter Day, the Sunday of the Resurrection. It begins after sundown on Holy Saturday. Fifty days long, the season includes the events of Christ's resurrection and ascension and the coming of the Holy Spirit on the Day of Pentecost (Whitsunday).

Easter is the principal feast of the Church Year.

The word "Easter" comes from Eostre, a Teutonic goddess whose name is associated with springtime, growth, and fertility. In most languages the name of the day is "Pascha," which means "Passover."

The Hebrew Feast of Weeks, itself called Pentecost, celebrating the end of the harvest, was held on the 50th day after the feast of unleavened bread. Pentecost, from the Greek meaning "50th," is the Christian feast that comes fifty days after Easter. The time between Easter and Pentecost is known as "The Great Fifty Days."

Easter Themes

The resurrection means that Christ has overcome death and in his victory has opened to us everlasting life. "Nothing can separate us from the love of God." Romans 8:39

New life—the Lord's new life in which we share—is the message of this season. Baptism (as the sacrament of new life) is an Easter theme. And as baptized Christians we take time during Easter to ponder what being members of Christ's body the Church means. We look at events in the Church's life—the sacraments, the accounts of ressurection and the postresurrection appearances of Jesus—to discover their meaning and what they tell us about how we as a community are to live the life of the Risen Lord. After the Lord is glorified in the ascension, he is present in a new way to the Church in the gift of the Holy Spirit at Pentecost.

Like the two who walked the Emmaus road with Jesus, we can know him in the breaking of bread at the Eucharist.

Great Words of the Easter Season

Alleluia!
Empty Tomb
Everlasting Life
He is risen!
Hope
Joy
Love

New Life (renewal)
Newly Baptized
Paschal Mystery
Promise
Reconciliation
Resurrection
Victory

Easter Through the Eyes of a Child

Jesus is risen from the dead! Easter has brought us everlasting life because of Jesus' resurrection.

God's love is stronger than anything, even death. Because of God's love, we do not have to be afraid of death.

Easter is about new life, coming from what we thought was death, that brings us unexpected possibilities and surprises.

We received new life at our baptism, and during Easter we think about what being baptized members of Christ's Church means in our lives.

Easter Worship Sentence for Young Children

LEADER: "Alleluia! Christ is risen!"

RESPONSE: "The Lord is risen indeed! Alleluia!"

LEADER—Arms at side; large arms-sweep, crossing arms in front of body; arms end in upraised position.

RESPONSE—Arms are outstretched above head and then lowered quickly and raised again in a large sweep that crosses arms in front of body. Arms end in upraised position.

Symbols and Traditions of Easter

Color—white for festival and joy.
The Paschal Candle—the darkness of death giving way to light and life; symbolizes Jesus passing over from death into life. Also symbolizes

the light of Creation, the pillar of fire that led the Israelites through the wilderness, the fire of Pentecost. *Pascha* is Greek for "Passover." The Paschal candle is lit from Easter through the Day of Pentecost. The year's date is carved into the candle to show that the Good News of Easter is for every age, including us today.

A customary Easter greeting that Christians have used for centuries:
LEADER: "Alleluia! Christ is risen!"
RESPONSE: "The Lord is risen indeed! Alleluia!"

The Great Vigil of Easter—held on Easter Eve during which the Paschal Candle is lit, the Exultet is sung or said, as many as nine Old Testament lessons recording God's saving acts in history are read, there are baptisms of new converts who commit their lives to Christ, and the Eucharist is celebrated to proclaim the Day of Resurrection.

Baptisms and confirmations have traditionally occurred in this season regarded as appropriate for the initiation of new Christians. Often these sacraments take place at the Great Vigil of Easter.

Feasting—breaking the fast of Lent with a feast is a sign of celebration and symbolizes the joy of the Christian community at Easter.

The empty cross—Christ the King is a sign of the victory of Easter.

Alleluias and the Gloria—joyful acclamations and sounds from the Easter community.

Butterfly—symbolizes resurrection or new life from a cocoon.

Egg—the Easter symbol from which new life emerges.

Pomegranate—a regal symbol, filled with red seeds which further symbolize life and fertility and the open tomb.

Ear of corn—as it bursts open we see the fertile new life within.

Easter Lily—symbol of purity and of beautiful new life.

Each Sunday is a "little Easter," reminding us as Christians of the resurrection, since it was on the first day of the week that Jesus rose from the dead. The joy of each weekly remembrance of the resurrection is always maintained, even during penitential seasons.

Local traditions—

Social Justice Themes for Easter

Third Sunday of Easter (Collect BCP 173/224–25)
"Open the eyes of our faith that we may behold him in all his redeeming work"

- actions of the Church and of individual Christians must be judged as to whether it is a redeeming or a demeaning work
- the healing ministry of the Church—societal healing as well as personal healing

Great Bible Stories for Easter

Old Testament Saving Acts of God:

- Noah's Ark and the Flood (Promise of Deliverance): Genesis 6:5–8:22
- The Passover: Exodus 12
- The Valley of the Dry Bones: Ezekiel 37
- Jonah and the Whale: Jonah 1–2:10

New Testament Parables of the Kingdom:
 The Grain of wheat: John 12:23–26
 The Talents: Matthew 25:14–30, Luke 19:11–27
 The Lost Sheep: Luke 15:1–7
 The Lost Coin: Luke 15:8–10
 The Prodigal Son: Luke 15:11–32
Postresurection Appearances of Jesus:
 The Road to Emmaus: Luke 24:13–35
 Thomas the Doubter: John 20:24–29
 Bribing the Soldiers: Matthew 28:11–15
 Command to Baptize: Matthew 28:16–20
 Conclusion of Mark: Matthew 16:9–20
 Jerusalem Appearance: Luke 24:36–53
 To Mary and Disciples: John 20:11–29

Great Hymns of Easter

Hail thee, festival day! (1st version)
The Strife is o'er, the battle done
He is risen, he is risen!

Opening Sentences of Scripture

Morning Prayer (BCP 39/77)

Antiphons

Morning Prayer (BCP 43/81)

Prefaces

Holy Eucharist (BCP 346/379)

Canticles

Invitatory: Christ our passover (Pascha nostrum) (BCP 46/83)
Canticle 7 or 21: We Praise Thee or You Are God (Te Deum Laudamus) (BCP 52/95)
Canticle 8*: The Song of Moses (Cantemus Domino) (BCP 85)
Canticle 9*: The First Song of Isaiah (Ecce, Deus) (BCP 86)
Canticle 18: A Song to the Lamb (Dignus Es) (BCP 93)

Prefaces

Holy Eucharist (BCP 346/379)

Prayers and Thanksgivings

Eucharistic Prayer A (BCP 362–63)
Eucharistic Prayer B (BCP 367–69)
The Collect for Sundays reminds us of the Easter nature of every Sunday as a weekly remembrance of Christ's resurrection (BCP 56, 69, and 98).
The Committal in the Burial Services reflects our confidence in the resurrection faith of Easter (BCP 485/501).

*particularly recommended for the Easter Vigil

A Service with Easter Themes

The Great Vigil of Easter (BCP 284)

Living the Easter Season at Home and in the Parish

Banners with the many symbols of Easter add to our mood of celebration and joy.

Remembering the "gardener" who met Mary on that morning of the third day, make a garden by the church or tend the church yard (John 20:15). Planting seeds or bulbs or trees reminds us of Easter's new life. Think about window boxes or perhaps "dish gardens" to be given to shut-ins or the elderly.

Make simple sculpture with wire and pliers to depict the joy of Easter, of resurrection, of new life.

An egg tree (decorated Easter eggs that have been "blown" and tied to a tree branch) can be used for a table centerpiece or classroom or home decoration.

Eggshell mosaics can illustrate an Easter story or symbols. Wash eggshells and glue them with white glue to make a design or picture on poster paper. Use plain or colored shells, adding color if desired, either before or after gluing. Mosaics could also be used to make Easter cards or glued on boxes as decorative gift containers.

Slides or photographs can be used to illustrate experiences of death and resurrection in our lives, either taken within the family or the congregation. As assignment to capture such Easter experiences could make photographers of any age alert to everyday events that express this season. A "live" or taped narration or musical background could accompany the presentation. A collage of magazine pictures could also portray this theme.

Easter cards could have potato-print stamps of Easter symbols on them. Mark the design on the cut end of half a potato and scrape the background away. Place the "stamp" on a sponge pad of poster paint or food coloring. Other card possibilities might be messages cut from any sort of lettering (newspaper or magazine letters, typed, stencils, or drawn or cut from all sorts of media, looped with yarn, ribbon, or string) or leaves or small flowers glued on to construction paper with an Easter message.

A triptych (perhaps made like a three-sided stained glass window) illustrating Palm Sunday, Good Friday, and Easter could be used in worship.

Eggs (or some other symbol of new life) could be made in a great variety of sizes from all sorts of materials and recycled scraps and hung in spots all over church or home for an Easter celebration.

Make kites with Easter symbols on them and enjoy flying them, remembering their symbolism of freedom and release.

Other local ideas

Ascension Day

Definition

The Ascension is celebrated 40 days after Easter, always on a Thursday, and recalls our Lord's being exalted by being taken gloriously up into heaven.

The Ascension is a major feast of the Church.

After Jesus' crucifixion and resurrection, our tradition tells us that he was seen for forty days, and that he then disappeared from the view of his disciples. Although they could no longer see him, they awaited the promised Spirit in Jerusalem.

Expectation Sunday is the name sometimes given to the Seventh Sunday of Easter which comes between Ascension Day and the Day of Pentecost. The name refers to the Apostles' expecting the promised coming of the Holy Spirit after Christ's Ascension.

Ascension Themes

The ascension is the third event in the cycle of crucifixion-resurrection-ascension in which Our Lord's life on earth culminates with the exaltation of his rising to heaven to live and reign gloriously with God forever.

The ascended Christ is Lord of all, and we are charged by Christ to be witnesses, evangelizing the world in his name: persons, institutions, systems, and nations.

In the ascension Christ has taken our human nature into heaven where as our Advocate, he intercedes for us continually to God.

Great Words of Ascension

Christ is Lord	Fulfillment
Crown of Life	Intercessor
Evangelize	King of Glory
Exaltation of human nature	Witness

Ascension Through the Eyes of a Child

Jesus is Lord in heaven, but he is also Lord in our hearts.

We do not have to be afraid about dying because Jesus has gone ahead to prepare a place for us in heaven with those who love God.

We know and feel real things we cannot see, like our parents' and friends' love.

Symbols of Ascension Day

Color—White, for festival and joy
   The King's crown—symbol of the reign of Our Lord Jesus Christ

Great Bible Stories for Ascension

The Ascension accounts: Matthew 28:16–20; Mark 16:14–20; Luke 24:36–53
   Jesus' Farewell Discourse (He prepares our place): John 14: 1–11

Great Hymns of Ascension

Hail thee, festival day! (Ascension version)
The head that once was crowned with thorns

ASCENSION IN THE BOOK OF COMMON PRAYER

Opening Sentences of Scripture

Morning Prayer (BCP 39/77)

Antiphons

Morning Prayer (BCP 43/81)

Prefaces

Holy Eucharist (BCP 347/379)

Prayers and Thanksgivings

Collect for Ascension Day (BCP 174/226)
Collect, Sunday after Ascension (BCP 202/254)
A Prayer of St. Chrysostom (BCP 59/72/102)
Collect: "Of the reign of Christ" (BCP 202/254)
4th Anthem (said before the Committal) in the Burial Service (BCP 483/501)

Living Ascension Day at Home and in the Parish

Illustrate and compare on opposite sides of a placard or paper or hanging—the Crown of Thorns and the Ascension Crown of glory, the Cross of Calvary and the empty tomb of Easter, the entry into Jerusalem where Jesus was greeted as a king and the ascension kingship of Christ.

Make a mobile illustrating the hymn "Crown him with many crowns."

Write a litany for the Prayers of the People, using the imagery of the whole world as part of God's kingdom. Perhaps "Your kingdom come, your will be done" or "we pray for your kingdom, Lord" could be repeated as the response.

Use one of the Royal Psalms (for instance Ps. 24 or Ps. 47) as the basis for a special procession, the intercessions, and/or artwork to illsutrate the ascension theme of Christ as king.

The Day of Pentecost (Whitsunday)

Definition

The Feast of Pentecost celebrates the day that the Holy Spirit came to the disciples as they were gathered together in Jerusalem. The Book of Acts tells us that the Holy Spirit was like the rush of a mighty wind, with tongues of flame like fire that rested on each person.

Pentecost is from the Greek meaning "fiftieth day," which was the Greek name for the Hebrew Feast of Weeks which fell on the fiftieth day after Passover. Christians took this name because this was the same day that the Spirit descended on the Apostles.

After Easter, Pentecost is the second most important feast of the Church.

Traditionally the Easter season has been a time of preparing for the rites of Christian initiation—Baptism and confirmation. The name of Whitsunday probably comes from the white robes worn on the day of baptism.

Pentecost Themes

Christ the Lord, crucified, risen, and ascended, is present to the Church through his Holy Spirit.

Pentecost is the great and glorious climax of the Easter Season when the Holy Spirit gives power to the Church through the Apostles to spread the Gospel to the ends of the earth.

Pentecost is the fulfillment of Christ's promise that God would send the Spirit to us to be with us always (John 14:16) to give power to God's people.

Pentecost is the birthday of the Church, of the New Covenant of a relationship with God given to the apostles, and through them to all believers.

The writer of Luke and Acts saw history as divided into three periods: the time of Israel and the Prophets (with John the Baptist as the last prophet); the time of Jesus' earthly ministry; and the time of the Church, which began at Pentecost and in which we are living now. Pentecost is the first event of the Church's history.

Great Words of Pentecost

Apostles	Indwelling
Breath (sign of life)	Inspiration
Dove	Mighty Wind
Empowered by the Spirit	New Covenant
Enthusiasm ([Greek] filled with	Proclaiming
the Spirit)	Renewal
Evangelism	Tongues of Fire
Gift of Speech	Witnesses

Pentecost Through the Eyes of a Child

God is always with us—this is his promise.

There is strength within us—the power of the Holy Spirit—like wind, which we can feel even though we cannot see it.

God wants us to help to bring all the people of the world, whom he loves, back to him. The Holy Spirit strengthens us to do this.

Pentecost Worship Sentence for Young Children

"The Holy Spirit makes us one people in the name of the Lord."

Arms outstretched above head, then lowered; hands touch shoulders and then take hands of people on either side.

Symbols and Traditions of Pentecost

Color—red, for the Tongues of Flame that signify the Holy Spirit.

The dove descending

indicates the presence of divinity

stands for the power of God working in people (see Matthew 3:16)

Tongues of Fire—a very ancient symbol for divine presence.

Mighty wind—felt and heard by the apostles; a symbol of the spirit (in Hebrew, Greek, and Latin, the words for "wind" and "spirit" are the same).

The Day of Pentecost (Whitsunday)   63

Hearing the lessons read in other languages at the Eucharist reminds us of the variety of languages spoken at the Pentecost experience.

Gathering for a Pentecost Vigil at night or early in the morning with the Order of Worship for the Evening. Instead of the *Phos hilaron* we substitute the Gloria in excelsis and a series of readings given on pages 896, 906, or 917 of the Prayer Book. The service concludes with Holy Eucharist.

Baptisms and confirmations are traditionally a part of both the Pentecost Vigil and Principal Services.

The Easter Alleluias are used at worship on this final day of the Easter Season.

Many worshippers wear red when they attend either the Vigil or Principal Service to signify the Tongues of Fire of the Holy Spirit.

Local traditions—

Social Justice Themes for Pentecost

The Day of Pentecost "...opened the way of eternal life to every race and nation..."

For study during Pentecost:

racism, sexism, and the other "isms" that deny God's love for all people

Great Bible Stories for Pentecost

The Tower of Babel—Confusion of Languages (Genesis 11:1–9)

The Mount Sinai event (Exodus 19, 20)

The Spirit resting on the 70 elders of Israel in the wilderness with Moses (Numbers 11:24–30)

Elijah/Elisha (II Kings 2:1–15)

Nicodemus (John 3:1–22)

The Pentecost Experience (Acts 2)

Great Hymns of Pentecost

Come down, O Love divine

Hail thee, festival day! (Pentecost version)
Come thou Holy Spirit bright (metrical version of Veni Sancte Spiritus)

PENTECOST IN THE BOOK OF COMMON PRAYER

Opening Sentences of Scripture

Morning Prayer (BCP 39/77)

Antiphons

Morning Prayer (BCP 43/81)

Canticles

Canticle 7 or 21: "We Praise Thee" or "You are God" (Te Deum laudamus) (BCP 52, 95)

Canticle 1 or 12: A Song of Creation (Benedicite, omnia opera Domini) (BCP 47, 88)

Canticle 19: The Song of the Redeemed (Magna et mirabilia) (BCP 94)

Prefaces

Holy Eucharist (BCP 347/380)

Prayers and Thanksgivings for Pentecost

The Collect for the Day of Pentecost is found on BCP 175/227 and an additional collect, "Of the Holy Spirit," is on BCP 200/251.

Eucharistic Prayer D (BCP 372, from the Liturgy of St. Basil.)

A collect "For the Unity of the Church" in the Holy Spirit is found on BCP 204/255.

Collects II (BCP 205/256) and III (BCP 206/256) pray for the Spirit's help in choosing suitable persons for ordained ministry and for the vocation of all Christians.

Services with Pentecost Themes

Vigil of Pentecost (BCP 175/227)

(Vigil begins with the Order of Worship for the Evening, BCP 109)

Ordination Rites (BCP 510–555)

The Dedication and Consecration of a Church (BCP 567)

Living the Day of Pentecost at Home and in the Parish

Have a birthday party for the Church with balloons and banners and a birthday cake, perhaps with doves on it. Think of red food—strawberries, punch.

Make a gift for everyone attending the Pentecost service. Cut tongues of fire from red, orange, and yellow felt to pin on the shoulder.

Balloons with messages of greeting and verses of Scripture can be released "to all the world." Give people your church address, asking them to contact you to find out where your messages traveled.

Have a celebration using wind: make and use kites and pinwheels, fans, wind chimes, mobiles that move in the breeze, toy sailboats for races, parachutes, scarves that trail in the wind, a model windmill.

Other local ideas

The First Sunday After Pentecost
Trinity Sunday

Definition

Trinity Sunday has been part of the Church Year since 1334, when it was designated in commemoration of the Doctrine of the Trinity—the total revelation of God in Christ: the Creator, God the Father; the Redeemer, God the Son; the Comforter and Sanctifier, God the Holy Spirit.

Our understanding of the Trinity is not based only on the Bible. It is found in the Creeds and has been part of the faith of the Church since earliest days.

Trinity Themes

The Creeds express our understanding of the three ways God is with us.

After the Crucifixion-Resurrection-Ascension cycle of Our Lord's life and the descent of the Holy Spirit to the Apostles at Pentecost comes the celebration of the full revelation of God in the three persons of the Trinity.

Trinity Through the Eyes of a Child

We know God when

we see God's creation going on in all the world

we learn of God's love for everyone from Jesus' life and teaching

we feel the power and strength of his Spirit which is always within us

Trinity is a time of excitement—joy—being alive—happy.

Symbols and Traditions of Trinity Sunday

Color—white, the color of joy
   Equilateral triangle—three in one
   Three interlocking circles—inseparability and unity
   In a blessing the Cross is signed in the names of the Father, Son, and Holy Spirit.
   We celebrate the Trinity in the Gloria in excelsis.
   All collects and many prayers end with ascription to the Holy Trinity.
   The Gloria Patri is added at the end of psalms and may be sung at the end of some canticles to bring a Christian emphasis to Old Testament writings, as they were appropriated for Christian worship.
   Other local traditions—

Great Hymns of Trinity Sunday

I bind unto myself today
Come, thou almighty King
Holy God, we praise thy Name

TRINITY SUNDAY IN THE BOOK OF COMMON PRAYER

Opening Sentences of Scripture

Morning Prayer (BCP 39/77)

Antiphons

Morning Prayer (BCP 43/81)

Canticles

Canticle 7 or 21: "We Praise Thee" or "You are God" (Te Deum laudamus) (BCP 52, 95)
Canticle 2 or 13: A Song of Praise (Benedictus es, Domine) (BCP 49, 90)

Prefaces

Holy Eucharist (BCP 347/380)

Prayers and Thanksgivings

The three Prefaces of the Lord's Day (BCP 377–78) summarize our understanding of the three Persons of the Trinity.

The Collects for Trinity BCP 176/228

An additional collect concerning the Trinity is found on BCP 199/251.

Services with Trinity Themes

Holy Baptism has a Trinitarian emphasis throughout. Notice especially the Baptismal Covenant (BCP 304–05), Thanksgiving over the Water (BCP 306–07), and the Baptism itself (BCP 307).

The prayer for renewal of the Baptismal Covenant said by the Bishop before Confirmation (BCP 309) refers to each of the Persons of the Trinity in their relationship to the life of a committed Christian.

The historic creeds that appear in the Prayer Book are sources of our understanding of the Trinity:

- The Apostles' Creed (BCP 53/96)
- The Nicene Creed (BCP 326–27)
- The Creed of St. Athanasius (BCP 864)

Living Trinity Sunday at Home and in the Parish

A banner or altar cloth can be made to express the theme of praise to the Trinity. A line from prayers or even an entire canticle could serve as the basis for these illustrations.

A triptych illustrating Creator, Redeemer, Comforter is a way to understand this doctrine visually. Perhaps a collage or mural or a bulletin board or slide show could portray participants' ideas of what each Person of the Trinity tells us about the nature of God and its meaning for our lives.

"The Grace" from II Corinthians 13:14 which appears at the conclusion of both versions of Morning Prayer and Evening Prayer is a text that lends itself to illustration, either by written means (poetry, sentence completion such as "The fellowship of the Holy Spirit makes me think of . . .") or visually (hangings, sculpture, murals, mobiles).

The Season After Pentecost

The twenty-nine Collects for the Sundays that follow Pentecost fall broadly under four important themes. Each theme is a statement of a basic Christian truth which applies to us at any age. As organizing principles for learning, these truths enhance the educational life of the Church community and make teaching more than mythology, because they are directly related to *our* lives.

THEME ONE: WE ARE GOD'S CHILDREN

Throughout his life on earth, Jesus told others about his Father, and did what he knew to be God's will for his life. Jesus served and honored his Father in all ways in his life and his death.

As we grow in faith and in years, to know ourselves as children of God calls for increasingly mature reponses; but the underlying truths are there for us at any age. Because we are God's children we trust him, we believe in him, we want to worship and serve him, and most of all we want to discover his will for our lives.

Propers Related to the Theme "We are God's Children"

Proper

1 (BCP 176/228)	10 (BCP 179/231)	18 (BCP 181/233)
2 (BCP 177/228)	11 (BCP 179/231)	20 (BCP 182/234)
4 (BCP 177/229)	12 (BCP 180/231)	21 (BCP 182/234)
5 (BCP 178/229)	14 (BCP 180/232)	22 (BCP 182/234)
7 (BCP 178/230)	17 (BCP 181/233)	25 (BCP 183/235)

THEME TWO: WE HAVE A PERSONAL RELATIONSHIP WITH OUR LORD JESUS CHRIST AND A MINISTRY OF LOVE TO OTHER PEOPLE

We have a relationship of faith with the living Christ and his mission through our prayers, the sacraments, and life in the community of the Church.

We know that Jesus is God. We know, too, that he is our brother. His incarnation, death, resurrection, and ascension are faith events for us, centered in the celebration of the Eucharist.

We try faithfully to respond to the commandment of Jesus Christ that we love one another as he has loved us.

Propers Related to the Theme of Our Relationship with Jesus Christ and One Another

Proper 9 (BCP 179/230); 15 (BCP 180/232); 27 (BCP 184/236); 28 (BCP 184/236).

THEME THREE: GOD CALLS US TO BE OPEN TO THE REALITY OF THE PRESENCE AND ACTION OF THE HOLY SPIRIT

We learn to understand the nature of the Holy Spirit as shown to us in the teaching of Jesus and elsewhere in the Bible.

We increase our ability to recognize the action of the Holy Spirit in our lives and in the world through prayer and thoughtful listening.

Propers Related to the Theme of the Action and Presence of the Holy Spirit

Proper 19 (BCP 182/233); 29 (BCP 185/236)

THEME FOUR: WE BELIEVE IN THE CHURCH AS THE BODY OF CHRIST IN THE WORLD, AND IN THE CHURCH'S MISSION

We believe in and work with the Church as it carries on its mission of bringing about the Kingdom of God in the world through prayers, service, and witness.

Propers Related to the Church and its Mission

Proper		
3 (BCP 177/229)	13 (BCP 180/232)	24 (BCP 183/235)
6 (BCP 178/230)	16 (BCP 181/232)	26 (BCP 184/235)
8 (BCP 178/230)	23 (BCP 183/234)	

OPPORTUNITIES FOR PARISH CHRISTIAN EDUCATION ON THE SUMMER SUNDAYS OF THE SEASON AFTER PENTECOST

The summer Sundays after Pentecost bring a great gift: TIME.

Time to do the important things that were put off because the year was to full to include them.

Time to plan ahead and to meet with leaders and teachers for the coming year.

Time to involve other leadership and give church school teachers who have worked through the past year more opportunity for their own spiritual growth.

Time for introducing special emphases (for instance, mission study, social justice issues, etc.)

Time for fun together as a whole parish or as smaller groups: picnics, cookouts, overnight camping trips, swimming parties, outdoor suppers.

STUDY AND PARTICIPATION POSSIBILITIES FOR A PARISH SUMMER EDUCATION PROGRAM

Because summer is the time for family vacations, summer camp, visits to friends and relatives who live in distant places, attendance is less regular and the patterns of parish Christian education usually change in summer.

If you haven't had much chance to explore such learning possibilities during the rest of the year, the summer Sundays after Pentecost provide rich opportunities for

Intergenerational participation and study where people of all ages come together to join in a variety of activities around a common theme. People of every age can be teachers and learners to each other.

Interest Centers planned around a central theme, set up in defined spaces in a large room or separated in smaller rooms, planned to include adults and children of all ages or prepared for children in specific groupings. Interest Centers might include:

- Arts activities, such as painting, lettering, clay modeling, stitching, mobiles, photography, film making

- Creative writing of all sorts or interviewing at church or elsewhere
- Simple creative drama, puppets, shadow plays or pantomime, choral reading, taping of sound effects
- Projects that will take several weeks, such as making banners, shields, research on a subject, displays, models or dioramas, field trips, outreach projects, nature or ecology activities
- Learning hymns or folk songs, exploring Christianity in the arts

A Vacation Church School for a specified period, two weeks, for instance.

Group-graded classes or other sorts of groupings that do not depend upon continuity of attendance.

Meeting in some different locations and at different times (such as outdoors, in each others' homes, at some place of recreation) for meals, overnight camping, or retreats.

PLAN THE SUMMER SESSIONS AROUND—

That *creative idea* there's never been time to try:

- Reenact the life of the early Christians. Build a house, make costumes, write scrolls, "St. Paul" can visit.
- Build a house or town of the Holy Land.
- Build a puppet stage for use all year.
- Cook and enjoy some foods mentioned in the Bible.
- Relive the entire church year, Advent to Pentecost, devoting one or two days to each season, depending on the time available. This is a possible summer camp program.

The Propers of Sundays after Pentecost
Concentrate especially upon the Parables of Jesus which appear in many propers.

Great Bible Stories
Story-telling, enhanced by simple creative dramatics, creative writing, painting, or other experiences.

Social Justice Issues

Identify issues in your community, the nation, or the world. Gather the information you need. Plan to invite local resource people who are involved in the issues. Develop sessions for research, field trips, films, keeping in mind the question: How can we as Christians respond to the situation?

A Mission Study

Information about the Church School Missionary Offering, The Presiding Bishop's Fund for World Relief, or The United Thank Offering may be obtained from the Henry Knox Sherrill Resource Center, Episcopal Church Center, 815 Second Avenue, New York, New York 10017. Information about *The Work You Give Us to Do: A Mission Study* may be obtained from the same address.

Episcopal Church Center Resources

Many study suggestions and resources are available from the Episcopal Church on issues of Aging, Alcohol and Substance Abuse, Evangelism, Public Concerns, Urban Concerns, and Domestic and World Hunger. For information contact the Henry Knox Sherrill Resource Center, Episcopal Church Center, 815 Second Avenue, New York, New York 10017.

The Calendar of the Church Year

(BCP 15–33)

Listings of days which are recognized as being of special importance in the Church Calendar:

1. Principal Feasts (BCP 15)
2. Sundays—all are Feasts of our Lord Jesus Christ (BCP 16)
3. Holy Days (BCP 16)
4. Days of Special Devotion (BCP 17)
5. Days of Optional Observance (BCP 17–18)

Ember Days

In each of the four seasons of the year, the Calendar of the Church designates a Wednesday, Friday, and Saturday as Ember Days. Ember Days occur in spring after the first Sunday in Lent; in summer after Pentecost; in autumn after September 14, Holy Cross Day; and in winter after December 13. The origin of the custom of setting aside these days and the meaning of "Ember" are hidden in long-ago Church history, but the days have continuing importance as traditional times for prayer for the ministry of the Church.

Rogation Days

Rogation Days (BCP 258–59) are observed on the Monday, Tuesday, and Wednesday before Ascension Day. "Rogation" comes from the Latin *rogare*, to ask. These days were originally set aside as times of prayer for bountiful harvests on land and sea. They have been expanded and are now times of prayer for commerce and industry and for the stewardship of creation as well.

The Propers note that they are for use on the traditional days or at other times.

Proper i—for fruitful seasons

Proper i i—for commerce and industry

Proper i i i—for stewardship of creation

Persons in the Calendar

Mary and Joseph; the twelve Apostles; the four Evangelists; Mary Magdalene; Stephen, who was the first martyr for Christ; James, the brother of our Lord; and the Archangel Michael are spoken of as "saints."

The Anglican communion in general accepts the New Testament understanding of "a saint of God" as meaning any Christian believer, and in this sense, any baptized Christian can be called "saint."

Most of the men and women whose lives and service the Church commemorates are not officially designated "saints," but are recognized as being great persons for whose lives we thank God and who are important in the tradition of the Church.

Lesser Feasts and Fasts

This volume gives proper collects, psalms, and lessons, and supplies short historical descriptions of the individuals and events.

Independence Day (July 4)

Definition

The Church recognizes the anniversary of the birth of our nation and our ongoing quest for liberty and justice.

Independence Day Themes

Freedom and liberation are human rights, allowing God-given gifts and potential to grow and develop.

Importance of the rights of people, who are all God's much-loved children.

The Fourth of July is a time to affirm our Christian call to justice and to pray for God's grace to assist and inspire and strengthen us.

Great Words of Independence Day

Freedom	Justice
Human family (brotherhood)	Liberation
Human rights	One nation under God
In God We Trust	Righteousness

Independence Day Through the Eyes of a Child

We celebrate the birth of our nation.

We continue to work for what is right for all people with God's help.

It is our responsibility to be good stewards of our nation's freedom, heritage, and resources.

A Symbol of Independence Day

United States Flag
Local traditions

Social Justice Themes for Independence Day

As citizens of this "nation under God," we are called to speak out against oppression of any person, including our fellow citizens, and to speak out for human rights in government, in institutions, in systems, and in social and personal life.

The Declaration of Independence offers us a way to examine and evaluate how faithfully we as a nation have brought about its promises for all our citizens.

A Great Hymn for Independence Day

God of our fathers, whose almighty hand

INDEPENDENCE DAY IN THE BOOK OF COMMON PRAYER

Prayers and Thanksgivings

Collect for the Nation	(BCP 207/258)
Collect for Social Justice	(BCP 209/260)
Collect for Social Service	(BCP 209/260)
Collect for Peace	(BCP 57/69/99)
Prayers for the National Life	(BCP 820–23)
Prayers for the Social Order	(BCP 823–27)
Prayers for the Natural Order	(BCP 827–28)
Thanksgiving for National Life	(BCP 838–39)
Prayer Attributed to St. Francis	(BCP 833)
Additional Prayers for Peace	(BCP 207/258, 815–16)

Historical Documents

Preface to the Book of Common Prayer, written at Philadelphia in October of 1789. Remember that the government of the Episcopal Church was organized by many of the same persons who established our nation's government.

Living Independence Day at Home and in the Parish

Enjoy a family or parish picnic with prayers, a reading of the Declaration of Independence, sharing stories of our forebears, and thinking of those places in the world where independence and freedom are being sought.

''Whose service is perfect freedom'' from the Collect for Peace (BCP 57/69/99) might serve as a theme for some sort of visual display, perhaps a collage or mobile showing examples of freedom in our lives and of freedom denied, using photographs and the daily newspaper. A litany and other prayers based on these topics can be used in worship, including asking God's help to stir and strengthen and renew us in bringing ''liberty and justice for all.''

Read the words of famous Americans and talk about how their lives have enriched our nation.

All Saints' Day (November 1)

Definition

On November first the Church remembers the saints of God—all faithful servants and believers. The day is seen as a communion of saints who have died and of all Christian persons.

All Hallows' Eve, October 31 (from which our Hallowe'en traditions come), All Saints' Day, and All Souls', November 2 (the Day of the Faithful Departed), are connected by tradition and are often celebrated together.

All Saints' Day Themes

We are always surrounded by a cloud of witnesses (Hebrews 12:1)—those faithful Christians who have died.

When we die, a new and everlasting life begins with God and others who have died before us.

The sacredness of persons is celebrated, remembering that they are all creations of God.

Baptism is the sacrament of Christian initiation which all Christian saints, living and dead, share as members of the Body of Christ.

The unique personality, gifts, talents, and experiences of every individual are given by God to be valued and used in the building of the Kingdom. Being good stewards of God's gifts means looking at our lives for clues about what we have to offer that will serve others in Christ's name. To become the people God intends us to be is to find our greatest happiness and deep fulfillment.

Great Words of All Saints' Day

Baptism
Cloud of witnesses
Communion of Saints

Eternity
Fellowship of the faithful
Gifts and talents

Kingdom of God   Obedience
Martyr   Saint
Ministry   Service

All Saints' Day Through the Eyes of a Child

We are all called to be saints, using our talents and lives to serve others, loving them as God loves us.

Famous saints are examples, showing us how to be followers of Jesus.

When we die, it is the beginning of a new life in which we join with others who have died and are close to God and Jesus.

Life in the Kingdom of God is life in a new way, without sorrow or pain, a life of joy.

Symbols and Traditions of All Saints' Day

Color—White for joy and festival

The Cross and Crown—for faithfulness and the Crown of Life (Revelation 2:10)

Reading the names of those who have died during the year, with prayers.

Local traditions—

Great Hymns for All Saints' Day

For all the saints who from their labors rest
Lift high the cross

ALL SAINTS' DAY IN THE BOOK OF COMMON PRAYER

Opening Sentences of Scripture

Morning Prayer (BCP 40/77)

Antiphons

Morning Prayer (BCP 44/82)

All Saints' Day (November 1)   81

Canticles

Canticle 7 or 21: "We Praise Thee" or "You are God" (Te Deum laudamus) (BCP 52/95)

Prefaces

Holy Eucharist (BCP 347/380)
   For the day commemorating a particular saint there are Prefaces on BCP 348/380–81

Prayers and Thanksgivings

For the Saints and Faithful Departed (BCP 838)
"O God, the King of saints…" (BCP 489/504)
Eucharistic Prayer D (BCP 372, from the Liturgy of St. Basil)
   Number 8 of the Concluding Collects (set at the end of the Prayers of the People) speaks of our being supported and surrounded by "your saints in heaven and on earth . . ." (BCP 395).
   Notice what the Anthem of Commendation in the Burial Service has to say about what life in heaven with the saints will be like (BCP 482–83/ 499).
   Prayer: For those who suffer for the sake of Conscience (BCP 823)

A Service with All Saints' Day Themes

A Form of Commitment to Christian Service (BCP 420)

Living All Saints' Day at Home and in the Parish

Look at the list of saints in the Prayer Book's calendar (pp. 19–33). Refer also to Lesser Feasts and Fasts (see Suggested References) to begin study of those whom the Church especially honors.
   Think about the many ways that people in any period of history (including our own) have expressed their love for God in service to others. Show the qualities of peoples' lives, whether famous or ordinary, in some visual form: a mural, a display, a mobile, an altar-hanging, a collection of objects that symbolize loving acts, a parade of costumed persons showing how they help or serve, or banners hung or carried in procession.

Many groups, especially Asian Americans, use All Saints' Day as an opportunity to remember and respect family members who are elderly or who have lived in other generations. This might be the occasion for telling about where our families have come from and lived, what their lives were like, and what values that we honor they have passed on to us.

Our names are symbols of who we are, and our Christian names tell who we are in our new life in Christ. A study of names and their meanings, of how our names show we are particular people loved individually and personally by God can help us see ourselves as particular saints of God whose lives are offered in loving service.

A design of everyone's name in a parish or family or other group can make an interesting All Saints' Day bulletin board, parish bulletin board cover, or other display. Photos made into a mobile (or shown in some other form) help convey our common Christian calling to be saints.

Biblical illustrations of Jesus' calling of the disciples, or invitations to others to follow him, can stimulate discussions and art or drama projects about how we and others can be followers today. Newspapers offer contemporary examples of such persons, many of whom provide genuine inspiration when we take time to notice and celebrate their often quiet and unnoticed acts.

Share with a family or other group the lives of persons (living or dead) whom you have always admired or wished to meet, saying what particularly attracts you to them and giving their names if you wish. Perhaps you might want to cite family and friends who have been influences or have helped you in some way. Writing such people a letter of gratitude, however simple, might be rewarding for everyone.

Visit a cemetery and read examples of how friends and loved ones have honored the dead on tombstones both now and long ago. Perhaps rubbings might be made from the tombstones, with appropriate permission. Making and discussing a "living will" is another way to render service to others. This might be a time to look at the memorials in your Church and talk about what they have meant.

Thanksgiving Day

Definition

The Church recognizes the traditional Thanksgiving holiday as a holy day for our land, life, and heritage.

Thanksgiving Themes

All our many blessings come from God's good creation.
    Christians are to live their lives in a spirit of thankfulness.
    We are to be faithful stewards of the earth as God's creation, given to us as a sacred trust.

Great Words of Thanksgiving Day

Blessings	Stewardship
Creation	Thankful hearts
Daily bread	

Thanksgiving Through the Eyes of a Child

We thank God for everything we have.
    We live our lives in a spirit of thankfulness for God's goodness.

Symbols and Traditions of Thanksgiving

The meaning of Eucharist is *Thanksgiving*.
    Feasting to share with others our celebration of thankfulness.
    Cornucopia—fruits and grains and the earth's bounty.
    We remember our heritage of struggle for freedom.
    Simple living, with respect for each other and the earth's resources, is a way to be thankful stewards of our blessings so that all may share them.

A Great Bible Story For Thanksgiving

Injunction for life in the Promised Land (Deuteronomy, Chapter 8).

THANKSGIVING DAY IN THE BOOK OF COMMON PRAYER

Prayers and Thanksgiving

The General Thanksgiving (BCP 58/71/101)
Litany of Thanksgiving (BCP 836)
The Thanksgiving Day Collect (BCP 194/246)
Rogation Day Collects (BCP 207/258)

Part II

THE LECTIONARY

The Lectionary—An Explanation

What is it?

A three-year cycle of readings from Holy Scripture to be read on Sundays and other Holy Days at all public services whether at the Liturgy of the Word in the Holy Eucharist or in Morning Prayer.

From the Latin *legere* (to read); the Lectionary is outlined on page 888 of the BCP, and it is followed by the Daily Office Lectionary beginning on page 934.

Why is it used?

Most of the Bible is read in a three-year span in this scheme which is followed by some eighty million American Christians, including all Episcopal Churches.

In its present form the Lectionary provides us the opportunity to see all of the Bible as the story of salvation through which God has spoken and continues to speak to us.

The Lectionary includes readings from the Old Testament, the New Testament, and the Apocrypha.

How is it arranged?

Appointed for each day are three readings and a portion of the Psalter. (Page 888 of the Prayer Book gives more complete instructions.)

The three years are designated A, B, and C, and always begin on the First Sunday of Advent. Year A is always a year evenly divisible by three.

The *first reading* is a lesson from the Old Testament or the Apocrypha. The theme will frequently relate to the Gospel lesson and/or the liturgical season. In Easter Season the first reading is from the Acts of the Apostles.

The *psalm* (or a portion of a psalm) relates to the first reading and/or the season of the Church Year.

The *second reading* comes from the New Testament, either from the epistles (frequently from Paul) or from other writings. Generally these readings do not relate to the other appointed lessons except on the major feast days. During Advent and Lent, however, they have a distinct tie to those seasons' themes.

The *Gospel reading* is from Matthew in Year A, from Mark in Year B, and from Luke in Year C. John's Gospel is used on important feast days, particularly during Lent, Holy Week, and Easter in every year. The Gospel is always read at the Eucharist and, though it may be the only lesson, at Morning Prayer.

What are the principal feasts?

Easter, Ascension, Pentecost, Trinity Sunday, All Saints' Day, Christmas, and the Epiphany are designated principal feasts in the Prayer Book. Their propers (readings specifically appointed for each of these days) will take precedence over all other readings or observances. Also taking precedence are the propers for Holy Name, the Presentation, and the Transfiguration when these days fall on a Sunday.

SUMMARY OF THE PSALMS AND READINGS FOR THE PRINCIPAL SUNDAY SERVICES OF ADVENT

THE FIRST SUNDAY OF ADVENT

Themes of the Collect (BCP 159, 211):

- God's grace to help us
- Good and evil (symbolism of light and darkness)
- the humility of Jesus, the Son of God who was born as a human baby
- Christ the Judge of the Living and the Dead at the end of the world
- Christ the giver of our immortal life

Year A

The Lesson   Isaiah 2:1–5
    The Prophet Isaiah looked ahead to a time when the people of the earth would learn God's ways, when God would judge his people, and they would give up war forever and live in peace "in the light of the Lord."

Psalm 122
    The song echoes the theme of the Lesson ". . . the tribes go up . . . to praise the Name of the Lord. For there are the thrones of judgment, . . ."

The Epistle   Romans 13:8–14
    Paul teaches that all the commandments are fulfilled when people love one another. He calls people to live in the full light of day; the time for leading new lives and being Christ's people is at hand.

The Gospel   Matthew 24:37–44
    Jesus tells his disciples of the judgment that will come without warning when the Lord returns.

Year B

The Lesson   Isaiah 64:1–9a
    A prayer for forgiveness, justice, and mercy.

Psalm 80 or 80:1–7
    A plea for restoration to life with God: "Show the light of your countenance and we shall be saved."

The Epistle   I Corinthians 1:1–9
    Paul writes to "all those who in every place call on the name of our Lord Jesus Christ," giving thanks for the grace of God that was given in Christ Jesus so that believers do not lack any spiritual gift as we wait for the coming of our Lord.

The Gospel   Mark 13:(24–32) 33–37
    Jesus tells Peter, James, John, and Andrew that the time of the coming

of the Son of Man at the end of history is known only to God; and he cautions all people to be alert and watchful.

Year C

The Lesson   Zechariah 14:4–9
After prophecies have been fulfilled, ". . . the Lord your God will come, and all the holy ones with him . . . and the Lord will be king over all the earth . . . ."

Psalm 50 or 50:1–6
God reveals himself in glory, come to judge both his loyal followers and those whose lives are evil.

The Epistle   I Thessalonians 3:9–13
Paul closes a letter to the people of the church in Thessalonica with thanks for the joy they have given him by their faith and love; and a prayer that when Christ comes again they may stand firm and faultless before him.

The Gospel   Luke 21:25–31
Jesus told of the signs of his coming again with power and great glory, and said that when these things begin to happen, people will know that the kingdom of God is near.

THE SECOND SUNDAY OF ADVENT

Themes of the Collect (BCP 159, 211):

- the Prophets, sent as messengers to preach repentance, and to bid God's people prepare for salvation
- our need for God's help to heed the warnings of the Prophets and give up our sins
- greeting with joy the coming of our Redeemer

Year A

The Lesson   Isaiah 11:1–10
The prophet promises that God will send a wise and understanding Judge who will be righteous and faithful in his decisions. Even animals

that are traditional enemies shall be at peace with one another. "They shall not hurt or destroy in all my holy mountain; for the earth shall be full of the knowledge of the Lord as the waters cover the sea."

Psalm 72 or 72:1–8
The expected Messiah will rule with righteousness and justice, and there will be peace to the end of time.

The Epistle Romans 15:4–13
Paul brings a message of hope to all people, and prays that the God of hope will fill the church in Rome with "all joy and peace and believing, so that by the power of the Holy Spirit you may abound in hope."

The Gospel Matthew 3:1–12
John the Baptist issues a strong warning to his hearers that they must repent and prepare for the coming of the Messiah.

Year B

The Lesson Isaiah 40:1–11
In these beautiful words we hear the promise of the coming of the Lord to a world where the way has been prepared, and in which the rough places have been made smooth.

Psalm 85 or 85:7–13
A song of hope and promise for the coming salvation.

The Epistle II Peter 3:8–15a, 18
Advent, when we are "waiting for and hastening the coming of the day of God," is a most appropriate time for us to think of the sort of persons we ought to be "in lives of holiness and godliness."

The Gospel Mark 1:1–8
As promised by the prophet Isaiah, John the Baptist appeared in the wilderness where he taught about the need for repentance. People confessed their sins and were baptized by John in the River Jordan. John told them that the Lord was coming and that he would baptize with the Holy Spirit.

Year C

The Lesson Baruch 5:1–9

"For God shall lead Israel with joy in the light of his glory, granting them his mercy and his righteousness."

Psalm 126

"The Lord has done great things for us." He has sent us a Savior and Redeemer.

The Epistle Philippians 1:1–11

Paul writes lovingly to the members of the new church in Philippi, praying that when the Lord comes to be our judge, they will be filled with the righteousness that comes through Jesus Christ.

The Gospel Luke 3:1–6

Luke places the ministry of John the Baptist in its context in history and reminds us that the prophet Isaiah had foretold that John would come to prepare the way of the Lord.

THE THIRD SUNDAY OF ADVENT

Themes of the Collect (BCP 160, 212):

- God's great power among us now to help us
- asking God's help to free us because our sin hinders us and makes us helpless
- God's grace and mercy

Year A

The Lesson Isaiah 35:1–10

Isaiah describes a time of glorious growth and healing for the people of Israel, when God will bring judgment and salvation, and his redeemed people will walk on the Holy Way.

Psalm 146 or 146:4–9

A song of praise for God's healing and hope, because God who feeds the hungry is faithful forever.

The Epistle   James 5:7–10

We are reminded that the coming of the Lord is at hand; to wait patiently without complaining about the people among whom we live; to remember the patience of the prophets who spoke in the Lord's name.

The Gospel   Matthew 11:2–11

When John the Baptist, who was in prison, sent his followers to Jesus to ask if he was the person whose coming had been promised, Jesus sent them back to John with words of healing and good news, very much like the healing described in the Lesson from Isaiah, leaving the implication that people must decide for themselves if Jesus is the promised one. Jesus spoke in strong words about John's ministry of preparation for Jesus' coming.

Year B

The Lesson   Isaiah 65:17–25

The prophet tells us of a time to come when God will create a new heaven and a new earth in which everyone will live to enjoy what they have worked for, and even the animals will live in peace together.

Psalm 126

A song of rejoicing in the Lord, in the expectation that the Lord will keep his promises, and do great things for his people.

or

The Magnificat—The Song of Mary   Luke 1:46–55   Canticle 3 or 15 (BCP 50 or 91).

The Epistle   I Thessalonians 5: (12–15) 16–28

Paul closes a letter to the church in Thessalonica with advice to live thankfully, to pray, to test everything, and to hold to what is good.

The Gospel   John 1:6–8, 19–28

Priests and Levites came from Jerusalem to ask John the Baptist who he was. They pressed him with questions. He told them that he was not the Messiah, nor Elijah, nor any other prophet. They wanted to know why he was baptizing. John replied, "I baptize with water, but among you stands one whom you do not know ...." John was aware that he had been sent to prepare the Way of the Lord.

The Advent Season   95

Year C

The Lesson   Zephaniah 3:14–20
   A call to rejoicing, celebrating the kingship of the Lord, whose care will provide security for his people. The future will be bright.

Psalm 85 or 85:7–13
   Expectation of salvation and promise of blessings to God's faithful people.

or

Ecce, Deus—The First Song of Isaiah   Isaiah 12:2–6   Canticle 9 (BCP 86).
   A song of praise for salvation, for the great one in the midst of you is the Holy One of Israel

The Epistle   Philippians 4:4–7 (8–9)
   "The Lord is at hand . . . and the peace of God, which passes all understanding, will keep your hearts and minds in Christ Jesus."

The Gospel   Luke 3:7–18
   John the Baptist warned the people that they must repent. When the people asked what they must do, he told them to share what they had, to collect no more than was due, to be content with what they earned.

THE FOURTH SUNDAY OF ADVENT

Themes of the Collect (BCP 160, 212):

- asking God, among us now, to purify our consciences
- the certain coming again of Jesus Christ
- asking God's help to make us prepared when Christ comes

Year A

The Lesson   Isaiah 7:10–17
   A sign in the time of Isaiah was an extraordinary event. The Lord through Isaiah offered to give a sign to Ahaz, King of Judah, and Ahaz refused, saying he would not expect God to perform some special feat

on demand. Isaiah responded that the Lord himself would give Ahaz a sign: A young woman would bear a son to be called Immanuel (God with us), and before the child was old enough to make decisions, the threat of the two kings would be ended.

Psalm 24 or 24:1–7
The king of glory will bless and reward those who live clean lives, who are honest in all things.

The Epistle   Romans 1:1–7
Paul introduces the gospel concerning the Son of God, and the blessings that come to those who are called to belong to Jesus Christ.

The Gospel   Matthew 1:18–25
Matthew's story of the birth of Jesus includes a quotation from the Lesson: "Behold, a virgin shall conceive and bear a son, and his name shall be called Emmanuel."

Year B

The Lesson   II Samuel 7:4, 8–16
The Lord gives the prophet Nathan a message for David, who reigns as king in Jerusalem. The Lord will establish David's descendants as a lasting kingdom to rule over his people Israel for ever.

Psalm 132 or 132:8–15
Described as a Royal Psalm, this may have been part of a coronation ceremony. "The Lord has sworn an oath to David; 'A son, the fruit of your body, will I set upon your throne.' "

The Epistle   Romans 16:25–27
At the close of Paul's letter to the Romans we find a benediction referring to "the revelation of that divine secret kept in silence for long ages but now disclosed, and through prophetic scriptures by God's command made known to all nations. . . . "

The Gospel   Luke 1:26–38
Jesus' miraculous birth is promised. This reading emphasizes what the child is to be named and the titles by which he will be described:

"Son of the Most High, the Lord God will give to him the throne of his father David, and he will reign over the house of Jacob for ever, and of his kingdom there will be no end."

Year C

The Lesson   Micah 5:2–4
"Bethlehem in Ephratha" was David's city. The ancient prophecy promises that a new ruler for Israel whose roots are far back in the past will come from this city.

Psalm 80 or 80:1–7
A cry to the Shepherd of Israel, that he will forgive and restore his people.

The Epistle   Hebrews 10:5–10
Jesus, through the offering of his body for our salvation, does away with ritual sacrifices and offerings that are made in obedience to law and creates a new sort of obedience.

The Gospel   Luke 1:39–49 (50–56)
Mary goes to visit her relative Elizabeth in the uplands of Judah. Elizabeth is expecting a child who is to be John the Baptist. Elizabeth is filled with joy at Mary's coming, and cries, "Who am I that the mother of my Lord should visit me?" The Song of Mary follows.

SUMMARY OF THE PSALMS AND READINGS FOR THE PRINCIPAL SERVICES OF THE CHRISTMAS SEASON

THE NATIVITY OF OUR LORD: CHRISTMAS DAY (DECEMBER 25)

Themes of the Collects (BCP 160, 161 and 212, 213):

- God makes us joyful with the yearly celebration of the birth of his only Son Jesus Christ.
- Because we gladly receive Jesus Christ as our Redeemer, we will trust him when he comes to be our Judge.

or

- God made this holy night bright with the true light of Jesus Christ.

- We pray that we who have known the mystery of that Light on earth may know him completely in heaven.

or

- God gave us his Son, who was born on this day to a pure virgin.
- We ask that we who are God's children by adoption and by his grace may be made new every day through his Holy Spirit.

Years A, B, C

Christmas Day I

The Lesson   Isaiah 9:2–4, 6–7
For Christians the words of the prophet are fulfilled by the coming of Jesus Christ. "Peace," as used in this reading means more than the absence of war. It points to the presence of Justice and righteousness.

Psalm 96 or 96:1–4, 11–12
A song of joyful praise to God—King, Creator, and Judge

The Epistle   Titus 2:11–14
The grace of God has dawned upon the world with healing for all persons; and Christians lead sober, honest, and godly lives while waiting for Jesus Christ to come in glory.

The Gospel   Luke 2:1–14 (15–20)
The story of the birth of Jesus.

Years A, B, C

Christmas Day II

The Lesson   Isaiah 62: 6–7, 10–12
The watchmen on the walls of Jerusalem are to pray constantly and give God no rest until his promises are fulfilled and salvation comes for Jerusalem. His people shall be called a holy people, redeemed by the Lord, long sought for, and not forsaken.

Psalm 97 or 97:1–4, 11–12
The Lord is king, and he will rule over all peoples.

The Epistle   Titus 3:4–7

God has saved us through baptism, sending the Spirit to us through Jesus Christ our Savior, so that we may become heirs in hope of eternal life.

The Gospel   Luke 2: (1–14) 15–20

After the angels who brought the good news of the Savior's birth had left them, the shepherds decided to go at once to Bethlehem to see for themselves what the Lord had made known to them. They found their way to Mary, Joseph, and the child, and told what they had heard about the child. The shepherds went back to their sheep, praising God.

Years A, B, C

Christmas Day III

The Lesson   Isaiah 52:7–10

A song celebrating the joyous return of the Lord and his people to the holy city.

Psalm 98 or 98:1–6

A song of praise for the final victory of God, who will judge the earth and establish justice.

The Epistle   Hebrews 1:1–12

God once spoke directly to his people, and after that he spoke to them through his prophets. Now he speaks to us through his Son, who has suffered for us and reigns at the right hand of God, supreme over the angels.

The Gospel   John 1:1–14

A hymn to the coming of Christ, who is described as the Word who was with God from the beginning, and through whom all things come to be. "And the Word became flesh and dwelt among us, full of grace and truth; we have beheld his glory, glory as of the only Son from the Father."

THE FIRST SUNDAY AFTER CHRISTMAS

Themes of the Collect:

- God has poured the new light of his incarnate Word upon us.
- We ask that this new light may shine in our lives.

Years A, B, C

The Lesson   Isaiah 61:10—62:3
The promise of a new name for Jerusalem given by God himself speaks of a Jerusalem redeemed and delivered according to God's promise.

Psalm 147 or 147:13–21
A hymn of praise of God, his power over nature and in history, his goodness to those who are faithful.

The Epistle   Galatians 3:23–25—4:47
Paul describes the law as having been the temporary guardian of God's children. Now that faith has come we are all children of God, baptized into union with Jesus Christ. Through the spirit of his son, we can call God by the name his Son uses, "Abba! Father!"

The Gospel   John 1:1–18

Christ is described as the Word who was with God from the beginning and through whom all things come to be. "And the Word became flesh and dwelt among us, full of grace and truth; we have beheld his glory, glory as of the only Son from the Father." No one has ever seen God. The only Son, who is with the Father, has made him known.

THE HOLY NAME OF OUR LORD JESUS CHRIST (JANUARY 1)

Themes of the Collect (BCP 162,213):

- God gave the holy name of Jesus to his Son as the sign of our salvation.
- We pray that God will make the love of Jesus Christ grow in every heart.

Years A, B, C

The Lesson   Exodus 34:1–8

The Lord reveals his glory to Moses, proclaiming his name and divine attributes. He is merciful and gracious, slow to anger, and abounding in steadfast love and faithfulness.

Psalm 8

God's name is exalted in all the world.

The Epistle   Romans 1:1–7

Paul writes about Jesus, who was descended from David, and shown to be the Son of God by his resurrection from the dead. His gospel is for all the nations.

The Gospel   Luke 2:15–21

Mary's son is given the name "Jesus," which in Hebrew means "The Lord saves."

The Second Sunday after Christmas

Themes of the Collect (BCP 162, 214):

- God created and restored the dignity of human nature.
- We pray that we may share the divine life of Christ, who humbly shared our human nature.

Years A, B, C

The Lesson   Jeremiah 31:7–14

The Lord promises to gather the people of the Northern Kingdom and restore them to their homeland, full of hope and joy.

Psalm 84 or 84:1–8

A hymn praising the Temple of the Lord, and proclaiming the happiness of the pilgrims as they come to worship.

The Epistle   Ephesians 1:3–6, 15–19a

Praising God who has given us all spiritual blessings in Christ, Paul thanks God for the people of the church in Ephesus, and prays that God will give them wisdom and vision to know the hope to which he calls them.

The Gospel   Matthew 2:13–15, 19–23
The flight into Egypt. Joseph and Mary escape from Bethlehem with the baby Jesus. They live in Egypt for a time, and later return to Nazareth when the danger is past.

SUMMARY OF THE PSALMS AND LESSONS FOR THE PRINCIPAL SERVICES OF THE EPIPHANY SEASON

THE EPIPHANY
THE MANIFESTATION OF CHRIST TO THE GENTILES (JANUARY 6)

Themes of the Collect (BCP 162, 214):

- By the leading of a star, God showed his only-begotten Son to the people of the earth.
- We know God by faith.
- We ask that God will lead us to his presence, where we may see his glory face to face.

Years A, B, C

The Lesson   Isaiah 60:1–6, 9
The promise of the New Jerusalem. Though darkness covers the earth and dark night the nations, Jerusalem will shine with the glory of the Lord. The wealth of the nations, gold and frankincense, will be brought to honor the Lord.

Psalm 72 or 72:1–2, 10–17
All kings shall bow down before him and all the nations do him service.

The Epistle   Ephesians 3:1–12
". . . the Gentiles are fellow-heirs, members of the same body, and partakers of the promise in Christ Jesus through the gospel." We all find unity in Christ.

The Gospel   Matthew 2:1–12

The story of the wise men from the East who came to Jerusalem to find the child born to be King of the Jews. Herod sends the wise men to Bethlehem, ordering them to come back to him with word of the child. They follow the star that they had seen in the East and are led to the child. These representatives of distant nations worship the child and offer gifts of gold, frankincense, and myrrh. They are warned in a dream not to return to Herod and go home by another way.

First Sunday After The Epiphany: The Baptism of Our Lord

Themes of the Collect (BCP 162, 214):

- At Jesus' baptism, God announced that Jesus is his beloved Son and anointed Jesus with the Holy Spirit.
- We ask that all who are baptized into Jesus' Name may be strengthened to keep the covenant they have made
- and fearlessly acknowledge Jesus as Lord and Savior.

Years A, B, C

The Lesson   Isaiah 42:1–9

Thus says the Lord: "Behold my servant, whom I uphold, my chosen, in whom my soul delights; I have put my Spirit upon him, he will bring forth justice to the nations."

Psalm 89: 1–29 or 89:20–29

God's promise of eternal rule for David the anointed king and his descendants.

The Epistle   Acts 10:34–38

Peter tells the household of the centurion Cornelius about Jesus. Peter has come to recognize that God has no favorites, but that God-fearing people from every nation are acceptable to him. Peter tells of Jesus' baptism and how God anointed Jesus with the Holy Spirit and with power.

The Gospel   Matthew 3:13–17

In Epiphany we celebrate the revelation of Jesus as our Savior. Matthew's gospel tells the story of Jesus'' baptism, John the Baptist's question, and Jesus' answer. A voice from heaven says, "This is my beloved Son with whom I am well pleased."

The Gospel   Mark 1:7–11

When he preached, John the Baptist said that a person greater than he would come who would baptize people with the Holy Spirit. Jesus came to John and was baptized by him in the River Jordan. After Jesus' baptism a voice from heaven declared that Jesus is God's Son.

The Gospel   Luke 3:15–16, 21–22

People wondered whether John the Baptist might be the Christ; but he told them plainly that someone was to come who would baptize with divine power and judgment. After the people had been baptized and Jesus had also been baptized and was praying, a voice came from heaven, saying: "Thou art my beloved Son; with thee I am well pleased."

SECOND SUNDAY AFTER THE EPIPHANY

Themes of the Collect (BCP 163, 215):

- Our Savior Jesus Christ is the light of the world.
- Through the light of God's Word and Sacraments, we ask that God's people may shine with Christ's glory
- and that Christ may be known, worshiped, and obeyed throughout the world.

Year A

The Lesson   Isaiah 49:1–7

The servant of the Lord speaks of his call and his mission to restore Israel; and of God's promise to become his strength. God will make his servant a light to the nations.

Psalm 40:1–10

A song of gratitude for deliverance; the righteous man values God's will above ritual sacrifice: "I love to do your will, O my God."

The Epistle   I Corinthians 1:1–9

Paul writes from Ephesus to the Christian congregation at Corinth, thanking God for the spiritual growth that has come to them in Christ.

The Gospel   John 1:29–41

John the Baptist tells of Jesus' coming to him as he was baptizing; and John bears witness that Jesus is God's Chosen One. Next day Andrew and another follower of John the Baptist go home with Jesus, and Andrew tells his brother Simon Peter, "We have found the Messiah!"

Year B

The Lesson   I Samuel 3:1–10 (11–20)

Eli recognizes that it is the Lord who is calling Samuel; and he tells Samuel to answer, "Speak, Lord, for your servant hears."

Psalm 63:1–8

"O God . . . eagerly I seek you." The presence of the Lord brings security and contentment.

The Epistle   I Corinthians 6:11b–20

Paul speaks against a misunderstanding of Christian freedom; and emphasizes that our bodies are a place of the indwelling Holy Spirit; and the spirit is God's gift to us.

The Gospel   John 1:43–51

Jesus calls Philip to be his disciple. Philip goes to Nathaniel and tells him that Jesus of Nazareth is the person who was spoken of by Moses in

the Law. Nathaniel questions that the promised Messiah could come
from the little town of Nazareth. Jesus surprises Nathaniel when they
meet and promises him a heavenly vision.

Year C

The Lesson   Isaiah 62:1–5
New names given by the Lord to Jerusalem point to God's favor, and
the relationship is compared to a marriage between God and his people.

Psalm 96   (1–10)
The Lord is King, and we are invited to join in a song of praise to
him.

The Epistle   I Corinthians 12:1–11
There are many varieties of gifts but the same Spirit. There are varieties of service, but the same Lord. These gifts are the work of the Spirit,
who inspires God's people to use them appropriately.

The Gospel   John 2:1–11
The miracle of water changed to wine at the marriage feast at Cana
points to Jesus' death and glorification when everything will be
transformed.

THIRD SUNDAY AFTER THE EPIPHANY

Themes of the Collect (BCP 163, 215):

- Our Savior Jesus Christ calls us, and we ask for grace to answer
  eagerly without holding back
- and proclaim the Good News of his salvation to all people
- and we and the entire world may perceive the glory of his marvelous
  acts.

Year A

The Lesson   Amos 3:1–8
Amos warns the people of Israel that the Lord will punish their wrong-

doing because he has chosen them from all the people of the earth to serve him. The Lord has spoken; and the prophet must reveal his words.

Psalm 139:1–17 or 139:1–11
Our Creator knows everything about us, even our innermost thoughts; and we are God's in special ways.

The Epistle   I Corinthians 1:10–17
Paul appeals to the members of the new congregation to be joined with one another in unity of mind and thought, and not to form cliques centered upon the person who introduced them to the faith.

The Gospel   Matthew 4:12–23
Jesus' ministry, preaching, and teaching; Simon Peter, Andrew, James, and John called to be disciples, "fishers of men."

Year B

The Lesson   Jeremiah 3:21—4:2
Israel's people plead for mercy and repent of the evil lives they have led. The Lord offers reconciliation.

Psalm 130
"Out of the depths have I called to you, O Lord"; "I wait for the Lord"; "With him there is plenteous redemption."

The Epistle   I Corinthians 7:17–23
Paul pleads with the congregations at Corinth to lead the lives to which God has called them and to recognize that one's place in life is not important to one's service to God.

The Gospel   Mark 1:14–20
Jesus' early ministry in Galilee, calling his hearers to repentance and God's forgiveness. Simon and his brother Andrew are invited to follow Jesus; and later Jesus calls the sons of Zebedee, James and John, who leave their father and come with Jesus.

Year C

The Lesson   Nehemiah 8:2–10

Ezra the scribe assembled the people of Israel in Jerusalem to hear the book of the law of Moses and to instruct the people in what was read.

Psalm 113

A song of praise to the Lord who raises the weak and the poor from their miseries.

The Epistle   I Corinthians 12:12–27

Paul reminds the congregation at Corinth that they are the Body of Christ and individually members of the Body. Every person is needed as part of that Body and no one can be discarded. They are joined as parts of the whole.

The Gospel   Luke 4:14–21

Filled with the power of the Holy Spirit, Jesus went back into Galilee. In the synagogue in Nazareth Jesus read from the book of Isaiah the good news of salvation. When he had read he closed the book and said, "To-day this scripture has been fulfilled in your hearing."

FOURTH SUNDAY AFTER THE EPIPHANY

Themes of the Collect (BCP 164, 215):

- God governs all things in heaven and earth.
- We pray earnestly that God will grant us his peace in our time.

Year A

The Lesson   Micah 6:1–8

God accuses his wayward people Israel, reminding them of all he has done for them and what he requires of them: "To do justice, to love kindness, and to walk humbly with your God."

Psalm 37:1–18 or 37:1–6

"Be still before the Lord and wait patiently for him."

The Epistle   I Corinthians 1:(18–25) 26–31

Paul reminds the Corinthians that God uses the powerless, the people of lowly origin, and even the simple and despised, to bring about his purposes. "Let him who boasts, boast of the Lord."

The Gospel   Matthew 5:1–12

In the opening words of the Sermon on the Mount (The Beatitudes) Jesus commends attitudes that are different from the values of the world, and promises that those who suffer for the cause of the right will experience the Kingdom of Heaven.

Year B

The Lesson   Deuteronomy 18:15–20

Moses called all Israel together and told them that God would raise up for them a prophet like Moses. God will reveal his will to the prophet, and the prophet will say only what God commands.

Psalm 111

A song of rejoicing for God's marvelous works. "The fear of the Lord is the beginning of wisdom."

The Epistle   I Corinthians 8:1b–13

Paul gives advice to the congregation at Corinth about eating the flesh of animals that have been sacrificed to idols. Since there is only one God, idols have no existence and the meat may be eaten. Nevertheless, it is better for those who understand that idols do not exist, and that the food may be eaten, to avoid eating this meat than to encourage other members to do what they believe is wrong.

The Gospel   Mark 1:21–28

Jesus and his disciples came to Capernaum, and on the sabbath Jesus taught in the synagogue. A man was suffering from an unclean spirit that recognized Jesus as the Holy One of God. The spirit obeyed Jesus' command to leave the man. "Even the unclean spirits obey him."

Year C

The Lesson   Jeremiah 1:4–10

Jeremiah is called to speak for God. He says, "I do not know how to speak; I'm only a young man." The Lord responds: "To everyone to whom I send you, you shall go; and whatever I command you, you shall speak . . . I have set you over nations and over kingdoms. . . ."

Psalm 71:1–17 or 71:1–6, 15–17

The psalmist prays for God's continuing protection.

The Epistle   I Corinthians 14:12b–20

Paul cautions the congregation at Corinth about the use of the gift of speaking in tongues. "He who speaks in a tongue should pray for the power to interpret."

The Gospel   Luke 4:21–32

The people in the synagogue knew Jesus' family and were puzzled and angered by his words. He spoke of Elijah and Elisha and their miraculous help to a widow and a leper who were not Israelites. The people led Jesus to a hill intending to throw him over the edge. He walked into the crowd and away from them, and went to Capernaum where he continued to teach.

FIFTH SUNDAY AFTER THE EPIPHANY

Themes of the Collect (BCP 164, 216):

- We ask God to release us from the bonds that are our sins
- and to give us the freedom of the abundant life shown to us in Jesus Christ.

Year A

The Lesson   Habakkuk 3:1–6, 17–19

Gratitude and trust in God in a dark and desperate time.

Psalm 27 or 27:1–7
"The Lord is my light and my salvation; whom then shall I fear?''
The psalmist expresses complete trust and a wish to be with the Lord
always. He implores the Lord for protection and promises to wait patiently for the Lord.

The Epistle   I Corinthians 2:1–11
The secret and hidden wisdom of God is not the wisdom of human
beings. God reveals himself through the Spirit.

The Gospel   Matthew 5:13–20
Jesus tells his disciples that they are the salt of the earth and the light
of the world and that he has come to fulfill the purpose of the law and
the prophecies. Only those who give their lives to God's will can enter
the Kingdom of Heaven.

Year B

The Lesson   II Kings 4: (8–17) 18–21 (22–31) 32–37
The account of the prophet Elisha and the woman of Shunem who had
a son as Elisha had promised. When the son was grown, he died. The
Shunammite woman journeyed to find the prophet, who was able to
restore her son to life through the power of God.

Psalm 142
A cry to God for help in deep trouble.

The Epistle   I Corinthians 9:16–23
Whatever he has to do to make it possible for people to hear and
understand the gospel, Paul will do. He tries to become all things to all
people for the sake of the gospel.

The Gospel   Mark 1:29–39
In the early days of Jesus' ministry there are accounts of his healing
many people who were ill or troubled. In today's gospel Jesus heals
Peter's mother-in-law.

Year C

The Lesson   Judges 6:11–24a

The angel of the Lord sends Gideon, who thinks of himself as unimportant and of his family as without power, to deliver Israel from the Midianites.

Psalm 85 or 85:7–13

A song of celebration of the Lord's salvation and a prayer for restoration and forgiveness.

The Epistle   I Corinthians 15:1–11

Paul reminds the congregation at Corinth that the scriptures are fulfilled in Christ's resurrection appearances. Paul speaks of five appearances and of his own experience of seeing the Lord.

The Gospel   Luke 5:1–11

Jesus tells Simon Peter to go out on the lake and put down the nets. Peter protests that they have fished all night and have caught nothing, but he will do what Jesus says. The nets enclose a school of fish and James and John in the other boat help with the enormous catch. They take their boats to shore, leave everything, and follow Jesus.

SIXTH SUNDAY AFTER THE EPIPHANY

Themes of the Collect (BCP 164, 216):

- God is the strength of those who trust him.
- We ask God to accept our prayers because we are weak human beings who can do nothing good without God.
- We pray that through the help of God's grace we may please him in our will and action as we keep his commandments.

Year A

The Lesson   Ecclesiasticus 15:11–20

It was God who created us in the beginning, and he has given us freedom of choice between good and evil.

Psalm 119:1–16 or 9–16
The psalmist is thankful for God's commandments, which point the way to life.

The Epistle   I Corinthians 3:1–9
Paul compares himself and other missionaries to workers in a field who plant and water, but the growth is from God.

The Gospel   Matthew 5:21–24, 27–30, 33–37
Jesus speaks of the inner dimensions of our actions and calls his followers to change their lives. "If you are offering your gift at the altar, and there remember that your brother has something against you, be reconciled to your brother and then offer your gift." Adultery is not only a physical act; and an oath made for emphasis may be blasphemy.

Year B

The Lesson   II Kings 5:1–15ab
Naaman, commander of the Syrian army, is a leper. He learns through a slave who had been carried off in a raid on Israel that there is a prophet in Samaria who can heal Naaman. The king of Syria sends Naaman to the king of Israel, who knows that he does not possess the power to cure Naaman and fears a plot. Elisha heals Naaman, who says, "I know there is no God in all the earth but in Israel."

Psalm 42 or 42:1–7
The psalmist cries out with longing to worship in the house of God.

The Epistle   I Corinthians 9:24–27
To emphasize the importance of discipline in the Christian life, Paul uses an analogy of runners who compete for a prize.

The Gospel   Mark 1:40–45
Jesus heals a leper and tells him not to say anything about his cure, but to go to the priest and make the offering that Moses commanded. The leper spread the word in spite of Jesus' command; and Jesus could not go freely into the towns but had to stay in the country with people coming to him from every direction.

Year C

The Lesson   Jeremiah 17:5–10
Draws contrasts between those who trust in their own strength and those who trust in the Lord.

Psalm 1
Contrasts between the righteous and the wicked.

The Epistle   I Corinthians 15:12–20
Paul raises the questions that surround Christ's resurrection. If there is to be no resurrection, we have no hope as Christians; but we know in fact that Christ was raised from the dead.

The Gospel   Luke 6:17–26
Jesus heals sick and troubled people who come to him. He teaches his followers that the hungry, the poor, and those who are reviled for his sake are blessed in God's eyes. Those who live in self-centered comfort will experience affliction.

SEVENTH SUNDAY AFTER THE EPIPHANY

Themes of the Collect (BCP 164, 216):

- God teaches us that without love, whatever we do is worth nothing.
- We pray that God will send his Holy Spirit to fill our hearts with love, which is his greatest gift.
- Without love, anyone who lives is counted as dead in the sight of God

Year A

The Lesson   Leviticus 19:1–2, 9–18
Through Moses God calls the people of Israel to live upright and charitable lives, to be righteous because God is righteous, loving their neighbors as themselves.

Psalm 71 or 71:16–24
The prayer of a person who has trusted God all through life. In old age, he asks for strength to continue to proclaim the righteousness of God.

The Epistle   I Corinthians 3:10–11, 16–23

Paul, still troubled by disruptions in the church at Corinth, says: 'Do you not know that you are God's temple and that God's Spirit dwells in you? You are Christ's, and Christ is God's.''

The Gospel   Matthew 5:38–48

Jesus teaches that it is not enough for us to love our neighbors who love us. We must love our enemies so that we may be children of our Father in heaven.

Year B

The Lesson   Isaiah 43:18–25

God speaks of his faithful care for his people Israel, though they have not responded to his love and forgiveness. ''I am he who blots out your transgressions for my own sake, and I will not remember your sins.''

Psalm 32 or 32:1–8

The psalmist thanks God for his forgiveness.

The Epistle   II Corinthians 1:18–22

God is faithful and consistent. All the promises of God find their ''*Yes!*'' in Jesus Christ.

The Gospel   Mark 2:1-12

Four men lower a paralytic through a roof into Jesus' presence. Jesus speaks to the paralytic, ''My son, your sins are forgiven.'' In Jesus' time physical and mental illness was thought to be the result of sin, and healing was related to forgiveness. Scribes who were in the room did not speak, but asked themselves, ''How can this man forgive sins?'' Jesus was aware of their unspoken questions. So that they might know he had authority to forgive sins, he said to the paralytic, ''I say to you, rise, take up your pallet and go home.''

Year C

The Lesson   Genesis 45:3–11, 21–28

Joseph declares his identity to his brothers and asks if their father is still living. Joseph believes that all that happened to him at the hands of his brothers was God's will and that God sent him to Egypt to preserve life there. His brothers return to their father, Jacob, with gifts, and Jacob says, "Joseph my son is still alive. I will go and see him before I die."

Psalm 37:1–18 or 37:3–10
The psalmist counsels patience, though the wicked seem to prosper. The Lord will uphold the righteous.

The Epistle   I Corinthians 15:35–38, 42–50
Further instruction to the people of Corinth about resurrection after dea*h. Paul explains that earthly bodies will be transformed into spiritual beings.

The Gospel   Luke 6:27–38
Jesus teaches: Love your enemies, do good to those who hate you, bless those who curse you, pray for those who abuse you. Do not judge and you will not be judged. Forgive, and you will be forgiven. The measure you give will be the measure you receive.

EIGHTH SUNDAY AFTER THE EPIPHANY

Themes of the Collect (BCP 165, 216):

- It is God's will that we shall give thanks for all things.
- Fear nothing but separation from God
- and turn over our troubles and worries to God, who loves us.
- We ask that we be kept safe from fears and anxieties that come from lack of trust in God
- and that no difficulties in our lives may hide from us the light of God's immortal love, shown to us in Jesus Christ our Lord.

Year A

The Lesson   Isaiah 49:8–18
The prophet, speaking to the people of Israel in exile in Babylon, promises that God will comfort and redeem Israel: God will never forsake his people.

Psalm 62 or 62:6–14
All that is left to the psalmist is a total trust in God.

The Epistle   I Corinthians 4:1–5 (6–7) 8–13

Paul describes in caustic terms his understanding of what it means to be Christ's servant. He describes his own life and that of Appollos as examples of service.

The Gospel   Matthew 6:24–34

Jesus urges his followers to trust in God to know their needs and to provide for them. Concern about material needs will draw them away from the fullness of life that God has promised.

Year B

The Lesson   Hosea 2:14–23

Israel is described by the prophet as a faithless wife whom God loves and will once more make his own. God will show his compassion, and the land will answer with grain, wine, and oil.

Psalm 103 or 103:1–6

A song of blessing to God for his grace and forgiveness.

The Epistle   II Corinthians 3: (4–11) 17—4:52

Paul tells the congregation at Corinth that God is calling his servants to be ministers of a new covenant in the Spirit of the Lord that gives life.

The Gospel   Mark 2:18–22

Jesus answers the criticism that his followers do not fast by comparing his time with his disciples to the presence of the bridegroom at a marriage feast.

Year C

The Lesson   Jeremiah 7:1–7 (8–15)

A warning sermon calls upon the people of Israel to amend their lives. The people come to the temple and repeat devout phrases while they continue to live in oppressive and unjust ways.

Psalm 92 or 92:1–5, 11–14

A song of thanks, comparing the faithful and righteous to trees that flourish in the courts of the Lord.

The Epistle   I Corinthians 15:50–58

Through our Lord Jesus Christ, God has given us victory over sin and death.

The Gospel   Luke 6:39–49

Jesus teaches the meaning of discipleship, and asks, "Why do you call me 'Lord, Lord,' and not do what I tell you." Those who hear his words and do them are like those who build on foundations of rock. Those who hear and do not do Jesus' words are like those who build without foundations.

THE LAST SUNDAY AFTER THE EPIPHANY

Themes of the Collect (BCP 165, 271):

- Before the suffering and death of Jesus, God showed the glory of his Son to his disciples on the holy mountain.
- We pray that we who see the light of the presence of our Lord through faith
- may be given strength to bear our crosses
- and be changed into his likeness from glory to glory.

Year A

The Lesson   Exodus 24:12 (13–14) 15–18

Moses receives the Ten Commandments on God's mountain, which was covered by a cloud. Moses enters the cloud, which is a sign of God's presence.

Psalm 99

A hymn in praise of God which speaks of experiences of Moses, Aaron, and Samuel. God is to be worshiped upon his holy hill, because he is the Holy One.

The Epistle   Philippians 3:7–14

Paul says that nothing in his life matters compared to the surpassing value of knowing and being known by Christ Jesus.

The Gospel   Matthew 17:1–9

In this account of the Transfiguration, Peter, James, and John see Jesus, shining with brilliant light, talking with Moses and Elijah. They hear the affirmation of the voice from the cloud; and are cautioned after the experience to tell no one what they have seen until the Son of Man is raised from the dead.

Year B

The Lesson   I Kings 19:9–18
God is present to Elijah on Mount Horeb in a "still, small voice," not in the wind, or the earthquake, or the fire. God tells Elijah to return to Damascus, describes Elijah's new work for God, and promises that there will still be people in Israel who have been faithful to God.

Psalm 27 or 27:5–11
The psalmist expresses his complete trust and his wish to be always with God.

The Epistle   II Peter 1:16–19 (20–21)
Peter describes the Transfiguration as an eyewitness.

The Gospel   Mark 9;2–9
The Transfiguration account from Mark's gospel.

Year C

The Lesson   Exodus 34:29–35
After Moses had received the Ten Commandments from God, his face shone with a radiant light. The people of Israel were afraid, and Moses veiled his face when he spoke with the people.

Psalm 99
The Lord is the ruler of the earth; he has established justice and righteousness; he has acted in the history of his people.

The Epistle   I Corinthians 12:27—13:13
With a variety of gifts, the congregation is the Body of Christ, and individually members of the Body. Unless one lives one's life in a spirit of love, nothing one does matters.

The Gospel   Luke 9:28–36

Luke's account of Christ's Transfiguration—Peter, James, and John saw his dazzling white clothing, his shining face, his conversation with Moses and Elijah, and heard the voice from the cloud proclaiming Jesus as the Son and God's Chosen.

SUMMARY OF THE PSALMS AND LESSONS FOR THE PRINCIPAL SERVICES OF THE LENTEN SEASON

THE FIRST DAY OF LENT: ASH WEDNESDAY

Themes of the Collect (BCP 166, 217):

- God hates nothing he has made.
- He forgives us when we are truly repentant.
- We ask God to give us new and contrite hearts.
- We are sorry for our sins and aware of our helplessness.
- We ask God to give us his perfect forgiveness through Jesus Christ our Lord.

Years A, B, C

The Lesson   Joel 2:1–2, 12–17

The day of the Lord is described as a time of darkness; '' and yet,'' the Lord says, ''even now turn back to me with your whole heart.'' The Lord will be gracious and compassionate if his people will return to him.

or Isaiah 58:1–12

God requires more than fasts made for private devotion. He requires that we share what we have with the hungry, take the homeless poor into our homes, clothe those in need, and be responsible in our families if we are to offer a fast acceptable to the Lord.

Psalm 103 or 103:8–14

A song of gratitude for God's fatherly care. He remembers that we are but dust.

The Epistle   II Corinthians 5:20b—6:10

''Now is the acceptable time;. . . now is the day of salvation.'' Paul calls the congregation at Corinth to be reconciled to God, and describes the incredible hardships he and other servants of God have endured for the sake of the Gospel.

The Gospel   Matthew 6:1–6, 16–21
Fasting, prayer, and support for the needy are not to be public demonstrations of piety. They are part of our private relationship with God.

THE FIRST SUNDAY IN LENT

Themes of the Collect (BCP 166, 218):

- God's Son was led by the Spirit to be tempted by Satan.
- We are assaulted by temptations from every direction.
- God knows our weaknesses.
- We pray that each of us may find God's mighty salvation through Jesus Christ our Lord.

Year A

The Lesson   Genesis 2:4b–9, 15–17,25—3–7
The second story of the Creation and Fall of man and woman in the garden in Eden. God has given us the choice of disobedience and awareness of good and evil so that we may come to recognition of our need for God's saving grace.

Psalm 51 (or 51:1–13)
A cry to God out of a sense of sin for renewal of a right spirit and the gift of a clean heart.

The Epistle   Romans 5:12–19 (20–21)
Paul contrasts human sin from the time of Adam with God's gift of salvation through Jesus Christ.

The Gospel   Matthew 4:1–11
After his baptism, Jesus was led by the Spirit into the wilderness. Hungry after a long fast, Jesus was tempted to prove that he was indeed the Son of God, possessed of supernatural powers. Rejecting every temptation, Jesus said to Satan, "You shall worship the Lord your God and him only shall you serve."

Year B

The Lesson   Genesis 9:8–17

God promises Noah that never again shall the Creation be destroyed by a flood; and designates the rainbow as a sign of divine reassurance to Noah.

Psalm 25 or 25:3–9

The Lord is faithful to those who keep his covenant.

The Epistle   I Peter 3:18–22

The water through which Noah and a few other persons were brought to safety corresponds to the water of baptism that brings salvation through the resurrection of Jesus Christ.

The Gospel   Mark 1:9–13

A description of Jesus' baptism and his acknowledgment by God as his Son, followed by a brief account in which Jesus, led by the Spirit, is in conflict with the powers of evil and receives the ministrations of angels.

Year C

The Lesson   Deuteronomy 26: (1–4) 5–11

Moses reminds the people that the first fruits of all their land produces belong to God in thanksgiving for their deliverance and for the good land to which God is bringing them. A liturgy that calls people to remember that it is God who hears our cries, sees our oppression, and delivers us.

Psalm 91 or 91:9–15

The Lord will protect and deliver those who trust in him.

The Epistle   Romans 10: (5–8a) 8b–13

If through faith we confess that Jesus is Lord and believe that God has raised Jesus from the dead, we will be saved. There is no distinction among people because the same Lord is Lord of all.

The Gospel   Luke 4:1–13

Following his baptism, the Spirit led Jesus into the wilderness. For forty days he had had nothing to eat and he encountered the devil, who tempted Jesus to take care of his own needs, to demonstrate supernatural gifts, and to become ruler of the kingdoms of the earth. Jesus answered the devil, "You are not to put the Lord your God to the test." The devil had run out of temptations, and he left Jesus, waiting to take up the contest at a later time.

THE SECOND SUNDAY IN LENT

Themes of the Collect (BCP 167, 218):

- We ask God, who is always merciful, to bring back those people who have strayed from his ways;
- to give them penitent hearts
- and firm faith in Jesus Christ.

Year A

The Lesson   Genesis 12:1–8
   The call of Abram (Abraham) to leave his country, his relatives, and his father's home to go to a country God would show him. God promised Abram that his decendants would become a great nation and through Abram all the families on earth would be blessed. Through Abram, God is still trying to restore the harmony of creation.

Psalm 33:12–22
   Human strength and earthly power cannot save; God's people trust him in all things.

The Epistle   Romans 4:1–5 (6–12) 13–17
   It was not through law that Abraham and his descendants were promised that theirs should be a great inheritance, but through faith. The promise is a matter of grace, so that it may hold true not only for those who are Abraham's descendants in law but for all who hold Abraham's faith in God.

The Gospel   John 3:1–17
   Nicodemus, a member of the Jewish Council, believing Jesus to be a teacher sent by God, came in the night to talk with him. Nicodemus wondered how it could be possible to be born again and to see the King-

dom of God. Jesus replied that this gift comes through water and the Spirit (baptism); and told Nicodemus that God loves the world so much that he gave his only Son so that everyone who has faith in him will have eternal life.

Year B

The Lesson   Genesis 22:1–14

Abraham's faith in God is tested, and Abraham demonstrates his readiness to sacrifice his son Isaac in obedience to God's command.

Psalm 16 or 16:5–11

God will guide those who trust in him throughout life and in death.

The Epistle   Romans 8:31–39

". . . neither death, nor life, nor angels, nor principalities, nor things present, nor things to come, nor powers, nor height, nor depth, nor anything else in all creation will be able to separate us from the love of God in Christ Jesus our Lord."

The Gospel   Mark 8:31–38

Jesus was preparing his disciples for his sufferings, rejection, and death. When Peter protested, Jesus reproved Peter and spoke to the people as well as to his disciples, and told them, "Anyone who wishes to be my follower must forget about himself, take up his cross, and come with me." Discipleship includes the possibility of really dying.

Year C

The Lesson   Genesis 15:1–12, 17–18

Abram (Abraham) grieved that he had no son to be his heir. God promised that he would have a son of his own and that his descendants would be as numerous as the stars in the sky. God made a covenant with Abram, in an ancient ritual, that his descendants should have the land between the river of Egypt to the Euphrates.

Psalm 27 or 27:10–18

The psalmist believes that no matter what troubles come to him, the Lord will be with him; and he will wait patiently for the Lord.

The Epistle   Philippians 3:17—4:1

Paul warns the church at Philippi that there are many people whose lives and values make them enemies of the cross of Christ, and pleads with the followers to stand firm in the Lord.

The Gospel   Luke 13: (22–30) 31–35

Jesus describes how difficult it will be to be saved—to enter the Kingdom of God. He scorns Herod's threat against his life, and turns his face to Jerusalem, where suffering and death are waiting for him. He grieves for the city of Jerusalem, which rejects and destroys the prophets sent by God.

THE THIRD SUNDAY IN LENT

Themes of the Collect (BCP 167, 218):

- God knows that we have no power to help ourselves.
- We ask him to keep us from anything that might hurt our bodies or our souls.

Year A

The Lesson   Exodus 17:1–7

The trust of the people of Israel disappeared in the face of the difficulties of their journey, and they were in open defiance of Moses' authority because they were thirsty. Moses cried to the Lord, believing that the people were ready to throw stones at him. God sent Moses to a rock which poured water when Moses struck it with his staff. Moses gave the place names that reflected the dissatisfaction of the Israelites and their putting God to the test.

Psalm 95 or 95:6–11

The psalmist warns people not to harden their hearts against God, as he speaks of the event of the Lesson and of God's anger with the people of Israel.

The Epistle   Romans 5:1–11

God accepts us on the basis of our faith. As sinners, we had lost our relationship to God; but we are reconciled with God through the death of his Son.

The Gospel   John 4:5–26 (27–38) 39–42

In Samaria, at Jacob's well, Jesus asked a woman of Samaria for a drink of water. She was surprised, because Jews and Samaritans would not drink from the same container, and it was contrary to custom for Jesus to talk with her. He revealed that he was the Messiah, and the woman marveled at him and went to tell the people of the city. They came to hear Jesus and acknowledged him to be the Savior of the world.

Year B

The Lesson   Exodus 20:1–17

Moses gave the people of Israel the Ten Commandments, God's requirements if they were to be in a covenant relationship with God and be his holy nation.

Psalm   19:7–14

The psalmist praises God's law and prays to be saved from secret faults.

The Epistle   Romans 7:13–25

Paul knows that the law is holy in itself, spiritual and admirable. Often when he wants to do right, only the wrong is possible for him. He is subject to God's law as a rational being, and is still a slave to the law of sin.

The Gospel   John 2:13–22

Jesus poured out the coins of the money changers and upset their tables in the temple . . . When challenged to show his authority, he said that if the temple were destroyed he would raise it in three days. The words are symbolic, speaking of Jesus' death and resurrection.

Year C

The Lesson   Exodus 3:1–15

God cared about the people of Israel in slavery in Egypt. He revealed himself to Moses in a bush that was burning without being burned up. God called Moses to lead the people of Israel out of Egypt. Moses asked by what authority he shall go to the Israelites, and God answered that he must tell them that Jehovah, the God of their forefathers, has sent Moses to them.

Psalm 103 or 103:1–11

The psalmist praises God for his goodness to Israel and to all persons. "He made his ways known to Moses."

The Epistle   I Corinthians 10:1–13

Paul reviews the experiences of the Israelites during the Exodus, and reminds the church at Corinth that baptism and the Eucharist do not in themselves protect people from sin and judgment. He promises that God will keep faith and will not allow us to be tested beyond our strength.

The Gospel   Luke 13:1–9

Jesus explains that the people involved in two disasters were not greater sinners than other people, since some might interpret these tragedies as God's judgment; but all are called to repent. The parable of the fig tree: a man had a fig tree, and looked for fruit on it and found none after three years. He told the man who tended his vineyard to cut it down. The man's response was: "Leave it one more year, and I will loosen the ground around it and give it fertilizer. If it bears fruit next year, well and good, if not, you can cut it down."

THE FOURTH SUNDAY IN LENT

Themes of the Collect (BCP 167, 219):

- Jesus Christ came to be the true bread that gives life to the world.
- We ask that God will always give us the bread of life.

Year A

The Lesson   I Samuel 16:1–13

David anointed king over Israel: The Lord, who had rejected Saul's kingship, told Samuel to go to Jesse of Bethlehem, because the Lord had chosen a king from among Jesse's sons. Samuel, like some other leaders chosen by God, was afraid to do as he was told, and went to Jesse reluctantly.

Samuel looked at seven of Jesse's sons, and the Lord had not chosen any of them. Jesse was told to send for his youngest son who was tending sheep. Samuel recognized David as the Lord's chosen; and he was anointed king by Samuel.

Psalm 23

Guided by the Lord, whom we often call the Good Shepherd, goodness and love follow the psalmist through his life.

The Epistle   Ephesians 5: (1–7) 8–14

Paul calls Christians to live in the light of Christ, which illumines everything, and to have no part in the deeds of darkness.

The Gospel   John 9:1–13 (14–27) 28–38

Jesus cures a blind man on the Sabbath, and is made known as the Light of the World who not only gives sight to eyes born blind but spiritual sight through baptism and faith.

Year B

The Lesson   II Chronicles 36:14–23

Through his prophets, the Lord had warned the chief priests and people of Judah that their way of life and defilement of the temple would have consequences. God gave them into the power of the Chaldeans, who killed without mercy and took as prisoners to Babylon those who had escaped death. After many years, Cyrus, king of Persia, proclaimed that God had commanded Cyrus to build him a house in Jerusalem, and that any of the people of Judah who were captive in Babylon might go to Jerusalem.

Psalm 122

A prayer for the peace of Jerusalem.

The Epistle   Ephesians 2:4–10

Our salvation, which is already accomplished, is God's gift to us through Christ Jesus, and not a reward for anything we may have done.

The Gospel   John 6:4–15

Jesus is the bread of the world: Jesus feeds the five thousand with five barley loaves and two fish; and the people hail Jesus as the prophet who was to come. Knowing that the people would want to hold him to proclaim him king, Jesus went into the hills to be alone.

Year C

The Lesson   Joshua (4:19–24) 5:9–12

After the people of Israel had crossed the Jordan into the Promised Land, they kept the Passover in Gilgal. They ate their unleavened cakes, and there was no more manna. That year they ate the food that had grown in the land of Canaan.

Psalm 34 or 34:1–8

The psalmist invites us to "taste and see that the Lord is good."

The Epistle   II Corinthians 5:17–21

For Christians a new world began with Christ. God has reconciled himself to us through Christ, and the message of reconciliation has been entrusted to us as Christ's ambassadors.

The Gospel   Luke 15:11–32

The parable of the Prodigal Son: Pigs are unclean to Jews, so everything about the son's work would have been inappropriate and distasteful. The son returns to his father, he is forgiven and received with honor; his elder brother who resents the attention the prodigal has received is gently rebuked but confirmed in his position.

THE FIFTH SUNDAY IN LENT

Themes of the Collect (BCP 167, 219):

- Only God can bring our self-will into order.
- We ask that God give us grace to love what he commands and to want what he promises,
- so that our hearts will center on the true joys of God's Kingdom.

Year A

The Lesson   Ezekiel 37:1–3 (4–10) 11–14

The prophet Ezekiel was shown by God a vision of a valley of bones that had been without life for a long time. God called upon Ezekiel to prophesy that the bones would become people of flesh who would have breath and spirit. The dry bones represented the people of Israel who were captives in Babylon, without hope, feeling severed from their roots. God sent Ezekiel to the Israelites to tell them that he would send his life-creating power to them and restore them to the land of Israel.

Psalm 130
The psalmist speaks out of hopelessness, and recognizes that his hope is in the Lord.

The Epistle   Romans 6:16–23
By God's mercy, Christians who were once the slaves of sin have become the slaves of righteousness. Freed from the commands of sin and given to the service of God, Christians live consecrated lives, and God's gift is eternal life in Christ Jesus.

The Gospel   John 11:(1–17) 18–44
The resurrection of Lazarus: The ultimate sign of Jesus as the Son of God who was to come to the world. Jesus said, "I am the resurrection and the life; he who believes in me, though he die, yet shall he live, and whoever lives and believes in me shall never die."

Year B

The Lesson   Jeremiah 31:31–34
God promises that he will make a new covenant with Israel and Judah, an internal covenant, not one recorded on stone tablets but written on people's hearts. "I will be their God and they shall be my people."

Psalm 51   (51:11–16)
A prayer for the gift of a clean heart and the renewal of a right spirit.

The Epistle   Hebrews 5: (1–4) 5–10
Named by God as his Son and high priest in the succession of Melchizedek, Christ's redemptive work is based on the obedience he learned through suffering. He became the source of eternal salvation for those who obey him.

The Gospel   John 12:20–33
Jesus speaks in words that reflect his obedience to his Father's will. He predicts his coming death: "When I am lifted up from the earth, I will draw everyone to myself."

Year C

The Lesson   Isaiah 43:16–21

The exile is over. The Lord tells his people that he is doing a new thing. He gives water in the wilderness and rivers in the desert so that his special people may drink and live.

Psalm 126

A joyous song of praise to the Lord. Salvation is described in terms of water in the desert.

The Epistle   Philippians 3:8–14

For Christ's sake Paul has lost everything that other people consider important, and he believes that nothing he has lost is worth considering so long as he may know Christ and the power of faith in Christ's resurrection and may share Christ's sufferings.

The Gospel   Luke 20:9–19

This harsh parable refers to a prophecy: "The stone the builders rejected has become the head of the corner"—the keystone of the kingdom to come.

SUMMARY OF THE PSALMS AND LESSONS FOR THE
PRINCIPAL SERVICES OF HOLY WEEK

THE SUNDAY OF THE PASSION   (PALM SUNDAY)

The Liturgy of the Palms

Year A   Matthew 21:1–11

In fulfillment of an ancient prophecy, Jesus enters Jerusalem riding on a donkey. Crowds of people spread their cloaks in the road and cut branches from trees to spread in his path. The people shouted "Hosanna to the Son of David," and other cries of praise and blessing. In Jerusalem people asked "Who is this?" and the crowd replied, "The prophet Jesus, from Nazareth of Galilee."

Year B   Mark 11:1–11a

Jesus and his disciples were close to Jerusalem when he sent two of his followers to bring him a colt that had not ever been ridden. Jesus mounted the colt, and the people carpeted the road with their cloaks, and cut branches to spread in his path. The people shouted "Hosanna! Blessed is he who comes in the name of the Lord!"

Jesus went into Jerusalem and entered the temple, but it was late in the day, and he went with his friends to stay at Bethany.

Year C   Luke 19:29–40

As Jesus reached the hill called Olivet, he sent two of his disciples to find a colt that no one had ever ridden. His followers threw their cloaks on the colt or cast them into the road as he passed by. In joy, the whole company of Jesus' disciples loudly sang praises to God in words that recall the angels' song at the time of Jesus' birth. Some Pharisees in the crowd wanted Jesus to reprove his disciples, and he answered that if the disciples were to be silent, the very stones would shout aloud.

Psalm 118:19–29

The Hosanna psalm. "Form a procession with branches."

THE SUNDAY OF THE PASSION   (PALM SUNDAY)

The Liturgy of the Word

Themes of the Collect (BCP 168, 229):

- God, in his love for all people, sent his Son to earth as a human being,
- to die a terrible death through which all people could see the example of his love and total obedience.
- We ask God to help us to understand the spirit in which Christ suffered and to share in his resurrection.

Years A, B, C

The Lesson   Isaiah 45:21–25

There is no other God; only in the Lord are righteousness and strength, in the Lord all the children of Israel shall triumph and glory.

or Isaiah   52:13—53:12

The suffering servant: Israel, the servant of God, has endured humiliation without protest because it was suffering for others. After suffering for all people, Israel will be given its rightful place. Christians think of the suffering of the servant as an early disclosure of Jesus Christ.

Psalm 22:1–21 or 22:1–11

The psalmist, whose sufferings are great and who feels forgotten, implores the help of the Lord.

The Epistle   Philippians 2:5–11

Paul describes Jesus, who was born as a human being and who took the form of a servant, obedient in all things, even to his death. God has greatly exalted Jesus, and all people who know him acknowledge that Jesus Christ is Lord to the glory of the Father.

The Gospel

Year A

Matthew 26: (36–75) 27:1–54 (55–66)

Jesus in Gethsemane; his trials; his sufferings and death.

Year B

Mark (14:32–72) 15:1–39 (40–47)

Jesus in Gethsemane; his trials; his sufferings and death.

Year C

Luke (22:39–71) 23:1–49 (50–56)

Jesus' prayers; his trials; his sufferings and death.

MONDAY IN HOLY WEEK

Themes of the Collect (BCP 168, 220):

- God's son Jesus Christ experienced pain before he found joy with his Father.
- He was put to death on the Cross before he entered into glory.
- We pray that we may find the way of the Cross to be the way of life and peace.

Years A, B, C

The Lesson   Isaiah 42:1–9

A poem that speaks of the relation between God and his servant. God speaks to introduce his servant, and the wording of the poem suggests that the servant is Israel.

Psalm 36:5–10

The psalm speaks of the priceless love of God, of his faithfulness, righteousness, and justice. The well of life is with God.

The Epistle   Hebrews 11:39—12:3

Thinking of us, God has made a better plan for a new covenant through Christ. With witnesses to faith around us like a cloud we must cast aside everything that would hinder us, and never lose sight of Jesus, who is the perfect expression of our faith. The joy that lay ahead for Jesus was to be seated at the right hand of God.

The Gospel   John 12:1–11

Six days before the Passover Jesus and his disciples came to the home of Lazarus, whom Jesus brought back from death. Martha served supper in Jesus' honor; and Mary spread pure oil of nard, a very expensive perfume, on Jesus' feet and wiped them with her hair. Judas Iscariot protested, and Jesus told him to let Mary keep the nard until she prepared him for his burial. He would not always be with them.

Because many Jews were putting their faith in Jesus, and wanted to see Lazarus who had been raised from the dead, the chief priests decided to kill Jesus, and Lazarus as well.

or Mark 14:3–9

TUESDAY IN HOLY WEEK

Themes of The Collect (BCP 168, 220):

- Through God, Jesus' shameful death on the Cross has become the means of life for us.
- We pray that we may glory in the Cross,
- and may willingly suffer shame and loss for Jesus' sake.

Years A, B, C

The Lesson   Isaiah 49:1–6

God's servant tells of the mission to which the Lord has called him, for which the Lord made him the restoration of Israel. But God intends his servant to do even more—''I will give you as a light to the nations, that my salvation shall reach to the ends of the earth.''

Psalm 71:1–12

The lament of one who is in deep trouble, who cries out for the Lord's help, and reminds God of his faithfulness in years past.

The Epistle   I Corinthians 1:18–31

Paul's description of the paradox of the Cross: What is folly to those on their way to ruin is the power of God to those on their way to salvation.

The Gospel   John 12:37–38, 42–50

In spite of the miracles Jesus has performed in their presence there were many who did not believe in him. Even among those in authority, there were many who believed in Jesus and would not admit it because they placed the highest value on their reputations.

Jesus said he had come into the world as light so that no one who had faith in him would remain in darkness. The Father who sent him commanded what he should say, and God's commandment is eternal life.

or Mark 11:15–19

WEDNESDAY IN HOLY WEEK

Themes of the Collect (BCP 169, 220):

- Our Savior surrendered his body to those who beat him and spit in his face.
- We ask God for the grace to accept our present sufferings joyfully, secure in the glory that will be revealed.

Years A, B, C

The Lesson   Isaiah 50:4–9a

The servant of the Lord speaks of his mission to listen like one who is taught. The servant offered his back to those who beat him, he did not hide his face from spitting, because the Lord God was with him.

Psalm 69:7–15, 22–23

A cry to God: ". . . I looked for sympathy, but there was none; for comforters, but I could find no one."

"They gave me gall to eat, and when I was thirsty, they gave me vinegar to drink."

The Epistle   Hebrews 9:11–15, 24–28

A new and greater sacrifice is offered by Christ, so that those whom God has called may receive the promise of the eternal inheritance.

The Gospel   John 13:21–35

Jesus predicts his betrayal by Judas Iscariot and gives Judas a piece of bread that Jesus has dipped in the common dish. When Judas had eaten the bread, Satan entered Judas. (The confrontation is with Satan.)

Jesus gives his friends a new commandment: That you love one another as I have loved you. By this everyone will know that you are my disciples.

or Matthew 26:1–5, 14–25

MAUNDY THURSDAY

The Church recalls the institution of our Lord's Supper on Maundy Thursday. "Maundy" comes from "mandatum" (Latin, meaning commandment) "A new commandment I give to you, that you love one another" (John 13:34).

Themes of the Collect (BCP 169, 221):

• On the night before his suffering Jesus shared a last meal with his disciples.

- He instituted the Sacrament of his Body and Blood.
- We pray that he will give us grace to receive the Sacrament thankfully, remembering that in these holy mysteries we have been given a promise of eternal life.

Years A, B, C

The Lesson   Exodus 12:1–14a
While the people of Israel were still in Egypt, the Lord gave Moses and Aaron directions for preparing and eating the Passover meal, and explained to them how he would judge Egypt and lead the people of Israel from their slavery.

Psalm 78:14–20, 23–25
The psalm tells of the hardships the people of Israel suffered after their deliverance from Egypt, and how the Lord gave them food and water for their needs.

The Epistle   I Corinthians 11:23–26 (27–32)
Paul tells the people of Corinth how he received the tradition he has transmitted to them, and how Jesus Christ had said, "This cup is the new covenant in my blood. Do this . . . in remembrance of me." As they eat the bread and drink the wine they proclaim the Lord's death until he comes again.

The Gospel   John 13:1–15
Jesus, in love and humility, washes his disciples' feet during his last Passover meal with them.

or Luke 22:14–30

GOOD FRIDAY

Themes of the Collect (BCP 169, 221):

- We ask God to look with kindness at us, his family,
- for whom our Lord Jesus Christ died on the Cross
- and lives and reigns forever with God and the Holy Spirit.

Years A, B, C

The Lesson   Isaiah 52:13—53:12

The song of the suffering servant of the Lord, sometimes thought of as Israel, humiliated and in pain like an individual. The servant bears his suffering without complaint because he is suffering for others. Christians think of the suffering servant, despised, wounded, yet bearing the sin of many, as an early disclosure of Jesus Christ.

or Genesis 22:1–18

or Wisdom 2:1, 12–24

Psalm 22:1–21 or 22:1–11

A cry for help from one who feels forsaken by God.

or Psalm 40:1–14 or Psalm 69:1–23

The Epistle   Hebrews 10:1–25

Christ has given us a new covenant by making for all time a single sacrifice for sin.

The Gospel   John (18:1–40) 19:1–37

Jesus' trials before the high priest and Pilate, his sufferings, and his death.

HOLY SATURDAY

Themes of the Collect (BCP 170, 221):

- The crucified body of Jesus was placed in the tomb and rested there on this holy day which was his Sabbath.
- We ask God that we may wait with Christ for the coming of the third day
- and rise with him to newness of life.

Years A, B, C

The Lesson   Job 14:1–14

The life of an individual is limited and its end is death. Job thought God was angry with him and Job wanted to hide from God in Sheol (the place of departed spirits in early Hebrew thought, where God was not present) for a period of time, rather than in death, from which he could not be waked.

Psalm 130

A cry to the Lord; one of the psalms in Christian liturgy that are used in times of mourning and as an expression of repentance.

or Psalm 31:1–5
A cry of deliverance and redemption.

The Epistle   I Peter 4:1–8

An appeal to Christians to accept the sufferings they endure for their faith, to pray and to love one another because "love covers a multitude of sins."

The Gospel   Matthew 27:57–66

After the crucifixion, Jesus was buried in the unused tomb of Joseph of Arimathea. On the morning after that Friday, the chief priests and Pharisees came to Pilate, asking that Jesus' grave be sealed and guarded for fear Jesus' friends would steal his body and tell people that Jesus had risen from the dead. Pilate told them that they could have a guard, and sent them to seal the stone.

or John 19:38–42

SUMMARY OF THE PSALMS AND LESSONS FOR THE PRINCIPAL SERVICES OF THE EASTER SEASON

THE GREAT VIGIL OF EASTER

See BCP 284 for a description of the Vigil. The service is found in BCP 285–95.

THE SUNDAY OF THE RESURRECTION (EASTER DAY)

Themes of the Collects (BCP 170, 222):

- God gave his only-begotten Son to the death of the cross for our redemption.

- By Christ's glorious resurrection we have been delivered from the power of our enemy.
- We pray that we may die daily to sin;
- that we may evermore live with him in the joy of his resurrection.

    or

- We pray that God will stir up in his Church the Spirit of adoption which is given to us in Baptism;
- that we, renewed in body and mind,
- may worship God in sincerity and truth.

    or

- Through Jesus Christ God overcame death and opened the gate of everlasting life to us.
- We pray that we may be raised from the death of sin by God's life-giving Spirit.

Early Service

Years A, B, C

The Lesson
One of the Old Testament Lessons from the Easter Vigil is used (BCP 288–91)

Psalm 114
A psalm of praise, telling how God saved Israel, and how the whole world enters into the joy of God's salvation.

The Epistle   Romans 6:3–11
All of us who have been baptized into Christ Jesus were baptized into his death; but if we have died with Christ, we believe that we shall also live with him.

The Gospel   Matthew 28:1–10
About daybreak on Sunday, Mary Magdalene and "the other Mary" went to the grave. There was an earthquake; an angel rolled away the stone and told the women that there was nothing for them to fear. Jesus was not there, he had risen as he said he would. The women were to see

the tomb for themselves and then go to tell the disciples that Jesus had been raised from the dead and would see them in Galilee.

Filled with joy, the women ran to tell the disciples. Suddenly Jesus was standing in the path. He greeted them, and they held his feet and worshiped him. Jesus told them not to be afraid, to take word to his brothers to go to Galilee, where they would see him.

Principal Service

Years A, B, C

The Lesson Acts 10:34–43

The centurion Cornelius (commander of 100 Roman soldiers) had been told in a vision that he should ask Peter to come to him and his relatives and friends to hear what the Lord had commanded Peter to say. The lesson, which is Peter's answer to Cornelius, is the beginning of the mission to the Gentiles. Peter speaks of Christ crucified and resurrected. Peter knows that the good news of the gospel is for all people.

or Exodus 14:10–14, 21–25, 15:20–21 (Year A); Isaiah 25:6–19 (Year B); Isaiah 51:9–11 (Year C)

Psalm 118:14–29 or 118:14–17, 22–24

A song of thanksgiving, rejoicing in the wonderful acts of God; and praising God that the stone the builders rejected has become the chief cornerstone.

The Epistle Colossians 3:1–4

Paul stresses our present sharing in the risen life of Christ.

or Acts 10:34–43

Year A

The Gospel John 20:1–10 (11–18)

Mary Magdalene finds the tomb empty and runs to tell Simon Peter and another disciple that the body of the Lord has been taken from the tomb. They see the linen cloths that had been used at the burial; and the other disciple sees and believes that Jesus has risen from the dead. (11–18) Mary Magdalene sees the risen Christ.

or Matthew 28:1–10 (see the Early Service)

Year B

The Gospel   Mark 16:1–8
Three women friends of Jesus came to the tomb early Sunday morning to find the huge stone that had been placed in front of the door rolled away. They went into the tomb and saw a young man, who told them that Jesus had risen. They were to tell his disciples that Jesus would go ahead of them to Galilee. The women were petrified with terror and said nothing to anyone.

Year C

The Gospel   Luke 24:1–10
Women followers of Jesus learned of his resurrection as very early Sunday morning they came, bringing spices. They found the tomb open and empty. "Two men in dazzling garments" suddenly appeared and asked the women why they were looking among the dead for someone who was living. Jesus had told them what would happen, how he would be crucified and must rise on the third day. The women went back and told the Eleven all they had seen.

Evening Service

Years A, B, C

The Lesson   Acts 5:29a, 30–32
Peter and the apostles were brought before the Sanhedrin (the ruling council of the Jews) and Peter spoke for them all before the high priest. What Peter said gives a concise summary of the apostolic tradition:
"The God of our fathers raised Jesus whom you killed by hanging him on a tree. God exalted him at his right hand as Leader and Savior, to give repentance to Israel and forgiveness of sins. And we are witnesses to these things, and so is the Holy Spirit whom God has given to those who obey him."

The Easter Season   143

or Daniel 12:1–3

Psalm 114
A psalm of praise telling how God saved Israel at the Exodus. The earth itself enters into the awe and joy of salvation.

or Psalm 136
This psalm is a litany in the Jewish liturgy, praising God's mercy in Creation, in the Exodus, in the wilderness, and his deliverance.

or Psalm 118:14–17, 22–24 (See the Principal Service)

The Epistle   I Corinthians 5:6b–8
Leaven (yeast), used in making bread, deteriorates and spoils; and to this day there is a Jewish household custom of throwing away all the yeast and all the bread baked with yeast before making the unleavened bread that is used at Passover. Paul speaks of Christ as the lamb offered as the Passover sacrifice; so we who observe the festival must be new like the unleavened bread of sincerity and truth.

The Gospel   Luke 24:13–55
Two of the disciples met Jesus on the road to Emmaus. Something kept them from knowing who he was. In response to his question they told him all that had happened in Jerusalem, and Jesus responded with scriptural passages referring to the Messiah. Night was coming, and the disciples invited Jesus to stay with them. He sat at the table and took bread and said the blessing, broke the bread and offered it to them, and in that act the disciples recognized Jesus. They knew him as we know him, in the words of the scriptures and the breaking of bread.

MONDAY IN EASTER WEEK

Themes of the Collect (BCP 171, 222):

- We celebrate the Paschal Feast.
- We pray to be made worthy of everlasting joy.

Years A, B, C

The Lesson   Acts 2:14, 22–32

Peter preaches a sermon on the crucifixion and resurrection of Jesus, in which he quotes a passage from the Psalms as a foreshadowing of the resurrection: "Thou wilt not abandon my soul to Hades, nor let thy Holy One see corruption." Peter and the other apostles are witnesses of the fulfillment of this in the resurrection.

Psalm 16:8–11

An expression of confidence in the Lord. The verses which Peter quotes in his sermon were taken to be a prediction of the resurrection.

or 118:19–24

A song of praise and thanksgiving to God for his mighty works: "The same stone which the builders rejected has become the chief cornerstone. This is the Lord's doing, and it is marvelous in our eyes." These verses were taken to be references to Jesus' work as Messiah.

The Gospel   Matthew 28:9–15

Jesus appears to Mary and Mary Magdalene after his resurrection. Meanwhile the chief priests and elders conspire with the soldiers who were guarding the tomb to spread the story that Jesus' disciples stole his body.

TUESDAY IN EASTER WEEK

Themes of the Collect (BCP 171, 223):

- In the resurrection of Jesus Christ God has destroyed death.
- We pray to share in the resurrection and abide in Christ's presence.

Years A, B, C

The Lesson   Acts 2:36–41

Peter preaches that God has made Jesus, whom the house of Israel rejected, both Lord and Christ. He calls on them to repent and be baptized, and promises they will receive the Holy Spirit. This promise is to everyone, near and far, whom the Lord calls to himself.

Psalm 33:18–22
The Lord watches over all who fear him, and will save them from death. "Let your loving-kindness, O Lord, be upon us, as we have put our trust in you."

   or 118:19–24

The Gospel John 20:11–18
Mary Magdalene, weeping in the garden outside Jesus' tomb, encounters the Risen Lord but does not recognize him. He calls her name and she knows him, but he tells her not to cling to him, as he has not ascended to his Father. She goes to the disciples and tells them she has seen the Lord.

WEDNESDAY IN EASTER WEEK

Themes of the Collect (BCP 171, 223):

- Jesus made himself known to the disciples in the breaking of bread.
- We pray that the eyes of our faith may be opened to see his redeeming work.

Years A, B, C

The Lesson Acts 3:1–10
Peter heals a beggar who has been lame from birth by calling on the name of Jesus Christ of Nazareth.

Psalm 105:1–8
A song of praise and thanksgiving to God for "the marvels he has done." "Give thanks to the Lord and call upon his name."

   or 118:19–24

The Gospel Luke 24:13–35
Two disciples meet the Risen Lord on the road to Emmaus, but they do not recognize him. In response to their account of the crucifixion, he

interprets for them the scriptural predictions of the messiah's suffering. At supper they recognize Jesus when he breaks the bread and serves it to them.

THURSDAY IN EASTER WEEK

Themes of the Collect (BCP 172, 223):

- The Paschal mystery has established the new covenant of reconciliation.
- We pray to be able to show in our lives what we profess by our faith.

Years A, B, C

The Lesson   Acts 3:11–26
Peter preaches to the crowd attracted by the healing of the lame man. He stresses the scriptural predictions concerning the messiah, particularly those indicating that the Christ would suffer. God raised up his servant, he says, and sent him to turn people from their wickedness.

Psalm 8
A song of praise for the wonders of God. "What is man? You have made him but little lower than the angels. You put all things under his feet."

or   114
A song of praise and thanksgiving for the Exodus. In the teaching of the New Testament, the Exodus is a foreshadowing of the resurrection.

or   118:19–24

The Gospel   Luke 24:36b–48
Jesus appears to the disciples and shows them—by inviting them to touch his wounds, and by eating a piece of broiled fish—that he is not a ghost, but a man of flesh and bone. He expounds the scriptures to them, showing that it was necessary for the Christ to suffer, but that he would also rise from the dead.

Themes of the Collect (BCP 172, 224):

- The Son of God has died for our sins and risen for our justification.
- We pray to God for help to turn us away from wickedness and to serve him purely.

Years A, B, C

The Lesson   Acts 4:1–12
Peter and John are arrested by the priests and Sadducees for preaching the gospel. In his statement before them Peter invokes the name of Jesus Christ of Nazareth, "the stone which was rejected by you builders, but which has become the head of the corner" (a quotation from Psalm 118).

Psalm 116:1–8
A song of thanksgiving for deliverance from death. The dying one is saved by calling on the name of the Lord.

   or   118:19–24

The Gospel   John 21:1–14
Jesus appears to the disciples beside the Sea of Tiberias. They are fishing and Jesus is on the shore. He tells them where to cast their nets, and then serves them breakfast when they come ashore.

SATURDAY IN EASTER WEEK

Themes of the Collect (BCP 172, 224):

- We thank God for delivering us from death.
- We pray that the love of Christ may raise us to eternal joy.

Years A, B, C

The Lesson   Acts 4:13–21
The rulers and elders of the temple command Peter and John to speak no more in the name of Jesus. But Peter and John refuse to stop speaking

of what they have seen and heard. The rulers release them without punishing them, because of their popularity.

Psalm 118:14–18
A song of praise to God for his triumphs. "I shall not die, but live, and declare the works of the Lord."

or 118:19–24

The Gospel Mark 16:9–15, 20
Jesus appears first to Mary Magdalene, then to two of the disciples, then to the eleven. He commands them to "Go into all the world and preach the gospel to the whole creation."

SECOND SUNDAY OF EASTER

Themes of the Collect:

- We pray that all the people who have been reborn into Christ's Body the Church
- may live their faith.

Year A

The Lesson Acts 2:14a, 22–32
Peter preaches a bold sermon on the street in Jerusalem on Pentecost, fifty days after Jesus' resurrection. Peter testifies to Jesus' resurrection, and says that all the apostles can bear witness to the risen Christ.

or Genesis 8:6–16; 9:8–16

Psalm 111
A song of praise for the Lord's grace and redemption.

or Psalm 118:19–24

The Epistle I Peter 1:3–9
God has given us new birth into a living hope by the resurrection of

Jesus Christ. Nothing can destroy our inheritance, which is God's continuing love.

   or Acts 2:14a, 22–32

The Gospel   John 20:19–31
   The risen Lord appeared twice to his friends. During his first appearance Jesus gave the power to forgive sins to the Church. Jesus affirmed the power of belief that does not depend upon physical evidence when Thomas's doubts vanish after touching the Lord.

Year B

The Lesson   Acts 3:12a, 13–15, 17–26
   Peter healed a crippled man in the name of Jesus Christ of Nazareth. People came running toward Peter and John; and Peter presented the essentials of the new Christian faith to them.

   or Isaiah 26:2–9, 19

Psalm 118:19–24
   A song of thanksgiving proclaiming that this is the day on which the Lord has acted to save his people.

   or Psalm 111

The Epistle   I John 5:1:6
   Faith in Jesus as the Christ makes it possible for us to accept other people as children of God. Faith leads to real Christian love.

   or Acts 3:12a, 13–15, 17–26

The Gospel   John 20:19–31 (See Year A)

Year C

The Lesson   Acts 5:12a, 17–22, 25–29
   The disciples continued with their healing mission and speaking and teaching the name of Jesus. The high priest and other leaders of the

Sadducees arrested and imprisoned the apostles. An angel opened the prison doors in the night and told the apostles to go to the temple and tell the people about the new life.

The high priest called together the ruling council of the Jews and sent to the jail to bring the prisoners before them. The prisoners could not be found until a man reported, ''The men you put in prison are in the temple teaching the people.''

The apostles were brought in and the high priest confronted them. ''You have filled Jerusalem with your teaching and you intend to make us responsible for this man's death.''

Peter answered for them all: ''We must obey God rather than men.''

or Job 42:1–6

Psalm 111
A song of praise and salvation.

or Psalm 118:19–24

The Epistle   Revelation 1:(1–8) 9–19
A disciple named John was on the Island of Patmos. ''Because I had preached God's word and borne my testimony to Jesus,'' John had a glorious vision of the risen Christ. John was told to write what he had seen of the present and of the future and to send it as a message from Christ to the seven churches in Asia.

or Acts 5:12a, 17–22, 25–29

The Gospel   John 20:19–31 (See Year A)

THIRD SUNDAY OF EASTER

Themes of the Collect:

- God's Son was known to his disciples in breaking bread
- We pray that God will open the eyes of our faith so that we may recognize Christ in all his redemptive work

Year A

The Lesson   Acts 2:14a, 36–47

At the close of his sermon on the Day of Pentecost, 50 days after Christ's resurrection, Peter told his hearers that Jesus, whom they had crucified, was the Lord and Messiah. They were "cut to the heart," and asked what they could do. Peter told them to repent and be baptized. He pleaded with them to save themselves, and three thousand were baptized that day. The apostles and those who had drawn together in faith praised God for their common life of prayer, meals, and teaching.

or Isaiah 43:1–12

Psalm 116 or 116:10–17

"I will lift up the cup of salvation;...I will offer the sacrifice of thanksgiving."

The Epistle   I Peter 1:17–23

A letter about the calling of a Christian, written to Christians who once were pagans, reminds them that the price of their freedom from their old lives was the blood of Christ. They have been born as a new people through the living and enduring Word of God.

or Acts 2:14a, 36–47

The Gospel   Luke 24:13–35 (See The Gospel for the Evening Service, Easter Day)

Year B

The Lesson   Acts 4:5–12

The apostles were brought before the Jewish authorities and asked, "By what power or by what name did you do this?" Peter, filled with the Holy Spirit, replied that if their question had to do with how a crippled man had been healed, it was by the name of Jesus Christ, whom the authorities had crucified and whom God had raised from the dead. Peter identified Jesus with the stone rejected by the builders that has become the keystone of the building (often mentioned in early prophecies) and the authorities with the builders. Peter said that only through Christ can we be saved.

or Micah 4:1–5

Psalm 98 or 98:1–5
A new song speaking of God's victory.

The Epistle   I John 1:1—2:2
This reading speaks of walking in God's light, of a common life which we share with the Father and the Son. God is light, and if we claim to share his life while we live in the dark, our lives are a lie. We can admit our sins, because God is just and can be trusted to forgive us.

or Acts 4:5–12

The Gospel   Luke 24:36b–48
The risen Lord comes to his disciples; they cannot believe the evidence of their senses. He invites them to touch him; he eats a piece of fish they had cooked. He explains that everything that has happened was part of God's intention for him, and that they are witnesses.

Year C

The Lesson   Acts 9:1–19a
A dramatic account of Saul's encounter with Jesus on the road to Damascus and Saul's conversion to the belief that Jesus is the Son of God.

or Jeremiah 32:36–41

Psalm 33 or 33:1–11
A song of praise, describing God as Creator and Ruler.

The Epistle   Revelation 5:6–14
John has a vision of the Lamb, symbolizing Christ, a Redeemer who receives the same sort of worship as God the Creator.

or Acts 9:1–19a

The Gospel　John 21:1–14

When Peter told a number of the disciples that he was going to fish in the Sea of Tiberias, the others said they would go with him. They fished all night and caught nothing. In the morning Jesus was standing on the shore, but the disciples did not know him. Jesus told them where to cast their net, and when they obeyed the net was so full of fish they had to tow it ashore. When Peter heard one of his friends say, ''It is the Lord,'' Peter couldn't wait for the boat to get there and plunged into the sea. A fire had been built on the beach, with fish cooking, and some bread. By now they all knew this was the Lord. Jesus took up the bread and gave it to them, and the fish as well. This was Jesus' third appearance to the disciples after he was raised from the dead.

FOURTH SUNDAY OF EASTER

Themes of the Collect:

- We ask God to grant that when we hear the Good Shepherd's voice
- we may know who is calling each of us by name
- and follow where he leads.

Year A

The Lesson　Acts 6:1–9, 7:2a, 51–60

The apostles called the people of the early Church together and asked them to choose seven men to serve the community in the distribution of food and in other ways, so that the apostles could devote themselves to prayer and the ministry of the word. Among those chosen was Stephen, who is described as being full of faith and of the Holy Spirit.

Stephen worked miracles among the people, and preached the gospel. He was falsely accused of blasphemy, dragged from the city, and stoned to death. As he was dying he cried out to Jesus to receive his spirit and to forgive his murderers. (Saul was present at Stephen's death.)

or Nehemiah 9:6–15

Psalm 23

The shepherd psalm of our pilgrimage of earthly life. The Lord will be our guide and host, and his unfailing love will be with us always.

The Epistle   I Peter 2:19–25

Christ suffered for us, and left us an example to follow. He bore our sins when he was crucified, so that we might die to sin and live to righteousness. By his wounds we have been healed. Although we have strayed, we have now come back to the Shepherd of our souls.

or Acts 6:1–9—7:2a, 51–60 (See the Lesson Above)

The Gospel   John 10:1–10

Jesus, teaching through a parable, describes himself as a shepherd who cares for his sheep, whose sheep follow him because they know his voice. He describes himself as the door of the sheepfold; those who enter through him shall be safe. He has come that people may have life in all its fullness.

Year B

The Lesson   Acts 4:(23–31) 32–37

A description of the communal life of the early Church in which all property was owned in common. It was not required for those who had property to sell it, but it was seen as the work of the Holy Spirit when this was done.

or Ezekiel 34:1–10

Psalm 23   (See Year A Above)

or Psalm 100

The Epistle   I John 3:1–8

The love that the Father has shown for us in Jesus Christ makes every Christian a child of God; but what we shall become as children of God remains a mystery.

The Gospel   John 10:11–16

Jesus describes himself as the Good Shepherd who lays down his life for his sheep. The Good Shepherd has other sheep (non-Jews) whom he must bring to the Father, and these sheep will also listen to his voice. The Good Shepherd lays down his life of his own free will in obedience to the Father, and he will receive it again.

Year C

The Lesson   Acts 13:15–16, 26–33 (34–39)
(Paul and his companions had journeyed as far as Antioch in Pisidia.) On the Sabbath they went to the synagogue, where the officials invited them to speak to the congregation.

Paul told the Jewish people that his message of salvation was for them. The people of Jerusalem had not recognized Jesus, but had condemned, crucified, and buried him without realizing that they were fulfilling all the prophecies about the Messiah. Paul and his friends were there to bring them the good news that God, who made the promise to their ancestors, had fulfilled it by raising Jesus from the dead.

or Numbers 27:12–23

Psalm 100
We are God's people and the sheep of his pasture.

The Epistle   Revelation 7:9–17
A vision of the saints and martyrs who are with God. The Lamb who is in the midst of the throne will be their shepherd and will guide them to the water of life, and God will wipe all tears from their eyes.

or Acts 13:15–16, 26–33 (34–39)

The Gospel   John 10:22–30
On a festival day Jesus was walking in the temple at Jerusalem. Jews asked him to tell them plainly if he was the Messiah. Jesus said he had told them, but because they were not his sheep they did not believe. His own sheep know his voice and follow him, and he gives them eternal life.

FIFTH SUNDAY OF EASTER

Themes of the Collect:

- Jesus Christ is the way, the truth, and the life.
- We ask God that we may truly understand this
- so that we may follow our Lord's example in the way that leads to eternal life.

Year A

The Lesson Acts 17:1–15

Paul and Silas made their way to Thessalonica. Paul preached in the synagogue for three Sabbaths, quoting scripture, proving that Jesus Christ had to suffer and rise from the dead. "And this Jesus," Paul said, "whom I am proclaiming to you, is the Christ." Some believed him and joined Paul and Silas; so did a number of God-fearing Greeks and many influential women.

A group of Jews made trouble in Thessalonica, and the congregation sent Paul and Silas to Beroea, where they were received eagerly. The Jews of Thessalonica followed them to Beroea and made trouble as before. Paul was escorted to Athens, where Silas and Timothy were to join him.

or Deuteronomy 6:20–25

Psalm 66:1–11 or 66:1–8

Praise to God who led his people out of Egypt.

The Epistle I Peter 2:1–10

Christians are described as chosen by God to be a royal priesthood, the people of God.

or Acts 17:1–15

The Gospel John 14:1–14

This reading is part of Jesus' last conversation with his friends. Jesus tells them to trust God and to trust him, and to be easy in their troubled minds; he is going to make it possible for the Father, the Son, and the disciples to be truly part of one another. Jesus says, "I am the way, and the truth, and the life; no one comes to the Father except by me." He also promises, "If you ask anything in my name, I will do it."

Year B

The Lesson Acts 8:26–40

A dramatic account of the baptism of an Ethiopian who is not named, described as a eunuch. He was the treasurer of the Queen of Ethiopia, going home from a pilgrimage to Jerusalem. The Spirit of the Lord sent Philip down the same road and told him to join the chariot of the Ethiopian, who was reading aloud a scripture passage from Isaiah.

The Ethiopian asked Philip to help him with the meaning of the passage, and Philip went on to give him the good news of Jesus. Along the road they came to water. The Ethiopian asked Philip to baptize him, which Philip did, and the Ethiopian went happily on his way.

or Deuteronomy 4:32–40

Psalm 66:1–11 (or 1–8)
Praise to God who led his people out of Egypt.

The Epistle   I John 3: (14–17) 18–24
Love must be genuine and must show itself in action. God has commanded us to believe in his Son Jesus Christ and to love one another as Jesus has commanded.

or Acts 8:26–40

The Gospel   John 14:15–21
Jesus tells his disciples that if they love him they will obey him, and he will ask the Father to give them the Spirit of truth to be with them always and to lead them. He promises that he will not leave them sorrowing; he is coming back to them.

Year C

The Lesson   Acts 13:44–52
On a Sabbath the almost total population of a town came to the synagogue to hear Paul and Barnabas. When the Jews saw the crowds they were filled with rage and violently opposed Paul's teaching. Paul and Barnabas told them that it was necessary to declare the good news to them first; and since they rejected it, Paul and Barnabas would turn to people who weren't of the Jewish faith. The non-Jews were overjoyed, and many became believers. Persecution of Paul and Barnabas continued; and they were finally driven from the area. The disciples were filled with joy and the Holy Spirit.

or Leviticus 19:1–2, 9–18

Psalm 145 or 145:1–9
A hymn of praise for the greatness and goodness of God.

The Epistle Revelation 19:1, 4–9
A vision of heaven in which a ''vast throng'' praises God and celebrates the marriage of the Lamb (representing Christ in Revelation). The bride of the Lamb is the Church.

or Acts 13:44–52

The Gospel John 13:31–35
Part of Jesus' final message to his friends. ''Where I am going you cannot come. I give you a new commandment: Love one another as I have loved you.''

SIXTH SUNDAY OF EASTER

Themes of the Collect:

- We ask God to fill our hearts with such great love for him
- that we may receive his promises,
- which are infinitely more than we can desire.

Year A

The Lesson Acts 17:22–31
Paul was in Athens, at that time the intellectual center of the western world. He began his message to the people of Athens with a comment that as he looked at the objects of their worship, which showed that they worshiped many gods, he saw an altar with the words, ''To an Unknown God.'' What they worshiped as unknown, Paul had come to proclaim. He went on to preach a concise and impressive sermon about God and our relation to him.

or Isaiah 41:17–20

Psalm 148 or 148:7–14
A song of praise to God who created everyone and everything in heaven and on earth.

The Epistle   I Peter 3:8–18

Peter calls the congregation to be filled with brotherly affection toward one another, which is the sign of the new birth; and to suffer for their faith if need be.

or Acts 17:22–31

The Gospel   John 15:1–8

Jesus tells his disciples that he is the true vine, those who believe in him are its branches, and his Father the gardener who prunes and tends the vine. These were familiar prophetic images to people in that day, and the union of vine and branches speaks powerfully of Christians being part of Jesus and of one another.

Year B

The Lesson   Acts 11:19–30

We learn how the early Church developed in the face of persecution and how Antioch came to be a center of the Faith. Barnabas brought Saul to Antioch, and together they taught a large number of people. In Antioch the followers of Christ were called Christians for the first time. Under the leadership of Saul and Barnabas the disciples in Antioch sent money to the believers in Judea.

or Isaiah 45:11–13, 18–19

Psalm 33 or 33:1–8, 18–22

A hymn of praise, describing God as Creator and Ruler.

The Epistle   I John 4:7–21

The command has come to us from Christ, that if we love God we must also love one another. "God is love" is not a way of defining God; it describes God's redeeming action through Christ.

or Acts 11:19–30

The Gospel   John 15:9–17

In Jesus' last lessons to his disciples, he calls them his friends and tells them that there is no greater love than that a man should lay down his life for his friends. He told them, "You did not choose me, I chose you," and also, "This is my commandment to you, love one another."

Year C

The Lesson   Acts 14:8–18

Paul and Barnabas were at Lystra, where Paul healed a man who had been crippled since birth. The crowds thought Paul and Barnabas were pagan gods who had come to them in human form and began to offer sacrifice to them. Paul and Barnabas spoke to the crowds, declaring their humanity, and the good news of the gospel; and narrowly escaped being worshiped as gods.

or Joel 2:21–27

Psalm 67

A hymn of praise for a generous harvest, asking for God's blessing.

The Epistle   Revelation 21:22—22:5

A vision of a city of light where there will be no need of the sun, and where the river of the water of life flows from the throne of God and of the Lamb. The Lord God will be their light, and God and the Lamb shall reign for ever and ever.

or Acts 14:8–18

The Gospel   John 14:23–29

Jesus, in preparing his disciples for his death, promises that the Holy Spirit will come to them. He gives them the gift of his peace, and tells them not to be afraid. He has told them in advance, so that when it happens they may have faith.

ASCENSION DAY

Themes of the Collect (BCP 174, 226):

- Jesus Christ ascended far above the heavens so that he might fulfill all things.

- We pray that God will give us faith to know that Jesus Christ is with his Church on earth,
- as he promised, to the end of the ages.

Years A, B, C

The Lesson   Acts 1:1–11
The reading tells about the close of Jesus' ministry on earth, how he appeared to his disciples and taught them, his promise that the disciples would receive power when the Holy Spirit came to them, and they would be Christ's witnesses not only where they were but to the most distant parts of the world. The disciples saw him lifted into the air until a cloud hid him from them.

While they were watching, two men in white robes stood near them and said, "This Jesus who was taken up from you into heaven, will come in the same way you saw him go into heaven."

 or Year A Daniel 7:9–14
  Year B Ezekiel 1:3–5a, 15–22, 26–28
  Year C II Kings 2:1–15

Psalm 47
A hymn celebrating God, King of all the earth. "God has gone up with a shout!"

 or Psalm 110:1–5
A song for the one who will reign at the Lord's right hand.

The Epistle   Ephesians 1:15–23
The writer gives thanksgiving and prays for the people of the church at Ephesus. He speaks of the infinite power of God in raising Christ from the dead to enthronement at God's right hand. God appointed Christ supreme head of his body the Church, which holds within it the fullness of Christ.

 or Acts 1:1–11

The Gospel   Luke 24:49–53
Jesus promised his disciples to send them his Father's promised gift.

He led them to Bethany and blessed them with his hands raised. As he blessed them he parted from them, and was carried to heaven. The disciples returned joyously to Jerusalem, praising and worshiping God.

or Mark 16:9–15, 19–20

Seventh Sunday of Easter (The Sunday after Ascension Day)

Themes of the Collect:

- We pray that God will send us his Holy Spirit
- to comfort and strengthen us
- and raise us to the place where our Savior has gone before us.

Year A

The Lesson   Acts 1:(1–7) 8–14
See the Lesson for Ascension Day, and add:
The disciples went back to Jerusalem to the upper room, where with Mary the mother of Jesus and his brothers they spent their time in prayer.

or Ezekiel 39:21–29

Psalm 68:1–20
A hymn praising God, "exalt him who rides upon the heavens" (v.4) and "you have gone up on high" (v.18).

or Psalm 47 (See Ascension Day)

The Epistle   I Peter 4:12–19
The significance of suffering as a Christian. Joyful acceptance of undeserved suffering shows trust in God.

or Acts 1:(1–7) 8–14

The Gospel   John 17:1–11
In his last hours with his friends, Jesus prays that God will reveal his glory through Jesus because Jesus has accomplished the mission he was sent to do. Jesus prays that God will protect the disciples.

Year B

The Lesson   Acts 1:15–26
Peter tells the brotherhood about the death of Judas. Peter realized that Judas' betrayal of Jesus was part of scripture that had to be fulfilled. Because Judas had been part of their group, they must choose someone to fill Judas's place among the twelve apostles. The choice fell upon Matthias, who had been with them from Jesus' baptism and had witnessed his resurrection.

or Exodus 28:1–4, 9–10, 29–30

Psalm 68:1–20   (See Year A)

or Psalm 47 (See Ascension Day)

The Epistle   I John 5:9–15
God has given us eternal life, and this life is found in Christ Jesus his Son. If we believe in the Son we truly have life. If we refuse to accept God's own witness to his Son, we will not have eternal life.

or Acts 1:15–26

The Gospel   John 17:11b–19
In his final time with his disciples, Jesus intercedes for them with the Father.

Year C

The Lesson   Acts 16:16–34
Paul and Silas were beaten and put in prison because Paul had healed a woman slave who was possessed by a spirit, and whose owners were angry at the cure. In the night, an earthquake broke open the doors of the prison and unfastened the bonds of the prisoners. The terrified jailer led Paul and Silas from the prison and asked what he must do to be saved. He and his whole family were baptized at once; and the jailer took Paul and Silas to his home.

or I Samuel 12:19–24

Psalm 68:1–20   (See Year A)

or Psalm 47   (See Ascension Day)

The Epistle   Revelation 22:12–14, 16–17, 20
In the prophecy of the last days, the Lord Jesus is envisioned as coming as Savior and Judge. He says, "Surely I am coming soon." The reading ends with a prayer that echoes down the centuries: "Amen. Come, Lord Jesus!"

or Acts 16:16–34

The Gospel   John 17:20–26
Jesus intercedes with God for future Christians as well as for the first disciples. The unity of those who believe will teach the world that Jesus' mission is from the Father.

SUMMARY OF THE PSALMS AND LESSONS FOR THE DAY OF PENTECOST

WHITSUNDAY

Themes of the Collects (BCP 175, 227):

- God has opened the way of eternal life to all races and nations
- by the promised gift of his Holy Spirit on this day.
- We pray that he will spread the gift throughout the world
- by the preaching of the Gospel
- so that it may reach every part of the world.

or

- God taught the hearts of his faithful people by sending them the light of his Holy Spirit.
- We pray that he will give us right judgment in all things
- and joy in the strengthening of the Holy Spirit.

Years A, B, C

The Lesson   Acts 2:1–11

The experience of the apostles on the Day of Pentecost, when the Holy Spirit filled them and they were able to tell the people of "every nation under heaven" in their own languages the great things God has done for us.

> or Year A   Ezekiel 11:17–20
> Year B   Isaiah 44:1–8
> Year C   Joel 2:28–32

Psalm 104: 25–37 or 104:25–32

A creation hymn through which praise is given for God's wonderful and benign order, the source of new life on earth. "You send forth your Spirit, and they are created."

> or Psalm 33:12–15, 18–22

The Epistle   I Corinthians 12:4–13

All Christians are brought into one body by baptism, in the one Spirit. We have been given varieties of gifts but the same Spirit. There are varieties of service, but the same Lord.

> or Acts 2:1–11

The Gospel   John 20:19–23

Late on the evening of that first Easter Sunday, the disciples were together with the doors locked because they were afraid of the Jews. Jesus came and stood among them and said, "Peace be with you!" When the disciples saw the Lord they were overjoyed. Jesus told them, "As the Father sent me, so I send you." He breathed on them, saying, "Receive the Holy Spirit." And the risen Lord, through the apostles, gave the power to forgive sins to the Church.

> or John 14:8–17

SUMMARY OF THE PSALMS AND LESSONS FOR THE SERVICES OF TRINITY SUNDAY

Themes of the Collect (BCP 176, 228):

- Through his divine power God has given us grace
- to confess a true faith
- and to acknowledge the glory of the eternal Trinity
- and to worship the Unity.
- We pray that God will keep us unwavering in our faith and worship
- so that at the end we may see him in his glory.

Year A

The Lesson   Genesis 1:1—2:3
The story of the Creation

Psalm 150
A doxology to end the Book of the Psalms, a song of joyous praise, closing with the words, ''let everything that has breath praise the Lord.''

or Canticle 2 or 13

The Epistle   II Corinthians 13 (5–10) 11–14
Paul will be coming to the church in Corinth for his third visit; he has had earlier conflicts with the converts in this place. Paul continues to hope, and urges the Christians in Corinth to live in love and peace with one another. He closes with the benediction that has become a familiar part of our worship: ''The grace of the Lord Jesus Christ, and the love of God, and the fellowship of the Holy Spirit be with you all.''

The Gospel   Matthew 28:16–20
Jesus appeared to the eleven disciples for the last time after they went to the mountain in Galilee where Jesus had told them to meet him. He came up and spoke to them, saying that he had been given complete authority in heaven and on earth. He directed them to go and make all nations his disciples; to baptize people everywhere in the name of the

Father, the Son, and the Holy Spirit; and teach them to live as he has commanded. Jesus closed with the promise: "I am with you always, to the end of time."

Year B

The Lesson   Exodus 3:1–6

Moses was tending his father-in-law's sheep near Horeb, the mountain of God, when an angel of the Lord appeared in a flame of fire in a bush. Moses went to see why the bush was on fire but not burned, when God called to him and he answered. God told Moses to stay back and to put aside his shoes because he was standing on holy ground. God said that he was the God of Moses' forefathers, and the God of Abraham, Isaac, and Jacob. Moses was afraid to look at God, and hid his face.

Psalm 93

The Lord is King; he controls the seas and secures order in the whole creation.

or Canticle 2 or 13

The Epistle   Romans 8:12–17

If we are led by the Spirit of God we are children of God. When we cry, "Abba! Father!" the Spirit bears witness that we are children and heirs of God and fellow-heirs with Christ. We must share the sufferings of Christ to share his glory.

The Gospel   John 3:1–16

Nicodemus, a member of the Jewish Council, believing that Jesus was a teacher sent by God, came in the night to talk with him. Nicodemus wondered how it could be possible to be born again and to see the Kingdom of God. Jesus replied that this gift comes through water and the Spirit (baptism) and told Nicodemus that God loves the world so much that he gave his only Son so that everyone who has faith in him will have eternal life.

Year C

The Lesson   Isaiah 6:1–8

Isaiah had a vision of the Lord high on a throne, surrounded by seraphim who sang praises to God. Isaiah felt guilty and unworthy to see the Lord. One of the seraphim, carrying a burning coal from the altar, touched Isaiah's lips and said, "Your guilt is taken away and your sin forgiven." Then Isaiah heard the Lord saying, "Whom shall I send? Who will go for us?" and Isaiah answered, "Here am I! Send me!"

Psalm 29
A hymn describing a tremendous thunderstorm, comparing the storm with the power and majesty of the Lord.

or Canticle 2 or 13

The Epistle   Revelation 4:1–11
A vision of the worship and praise of God the Creator in heaven.

The Gospel   John 16:(5–11) 12–15
In one of Jesus' last conversations with his friends, he has told them that he will be leaving them. None of them has asked where he is going, all are deep in grief at what he has told them. Jesus says that if he does not go, the Spirit of truth whom he will send them from the Father will not come to them. The Spirit of truth will judge the sin of the world, affirm that Jesus is with the Father, and prove that God condemns the powers of evil.

THE SEASON AFTER PENTECOST

PROPER 1:

The Sunday closest to May 11

Themes of the Collect:

- We ask God to remember what he has created in us and not what we deserve.
- Since God has called us to serve him, we ask him to make us worthy of our calling.

Year A

The Lesson   Ecclesiasticus 15:11–20
It was God who created us in the beginning, and he has given us freedom of choice between good and evil.

Psalm 119:1–16 or 119:9–16
The psalmist is thankful for God's commandments, which point the way to live.

The Epistle   1 Corinthians 3:1–9
Paul compares himself and other missionaries to workers in a field who plant and water, but the growth is from God.

The Gospel   Matthew 5:21–24, 27–30, 33–37
Jesus speaks of the inner dimensions of our actions and calls his followers to change their lives. "If you are offering your gift at the altar, and there remember that your brother has something against you, be reconciled to your brother and then offer your gift." Adultery is not only a physical act; and an oath made for emphasis may be blasphemy.

Year B

The Lesson   2 Kings 5:1–15ab
Naaman, commander of the Syrian army, is a leper. He learns through a slave who had been carried off in a raid on Israel that there is a prophet in Samaria who can heal Naaman. The King of Syria sends Naaman to the King of Israel who knows that he does not possess the power to cure Naaman and fears a plot. Elisha heals Naaman, who says, "I know there is no God in all the earth but in Israel."

Psalm 42 or 42:1–7
The psalmist cries out with longing to worship in the house of God.

The Epistle   1 Corinthians 9:24–27
To emphasize the importance of discipline in the Christian life, Paul uses an analogy of runners who compete for a prize.

The Gospel   Mark 1:40–45
Jesus heals a leper and tells him not to say anything about his cure but to go to the priest and make the offering that Moses commanded. The

leper spread the word in spite of Jesus' request, and Jesus could no longer go freely into the towns but had to stay in the country, with people coming to him from every direction.

Year C

The Lesson   Jeremiah 17:5–10
Draws contrasts between those who trust in their own strength and those who trust in the Lord.

Psalm 1
The psalmist contrasts the righteous and the wicked.

The Epistle   1 Corinthians 15:12–20
Paul raises the questions that surround Christ's resurrection. If there is to be no resurrection, we have only vain hope as Christians; but we know in fact that Christ was raised from the dead.

The Gospel   Luke 6:17–26
Jesus heals sick and troubled people who come to him. He teaches his followers that the hungry, the poor, and those who are reviled for his sake are blessed in God's eyes. Those who live in self-centered comfort will experience affliction.

PROPER 2:

The Sunday closest to May 18

Themes of the Collect:

- We ask God in his mercy and goodness to keep us from everything that might hurt us so that being ready in mind and body
- we may attain the things that are part of God's purpose for our lives with free hearts.

Year A

The Lesson   Leviticus 19:1–2, 9–18
Through Moses God calls the people of Israel to live upright and

charitable lives, to be righteous because God is righteous, loving their neighbors as themselves.

Psalm 71 or 71:16–24
The prayer of a person who has trusted God all through life. In old age he asks for strength to continue to proclaim the righteousness of God.

The Epistle   1 Corinthians 3:10–11, 16–23
Paul, still troubled by disruptions in the church at Corinth, says: "Do you not know that you are God's temple and that God's Spirit dwells in you? You are Christ's, and Christ is God's."

The Gospel   Matthew 5:38–48
Jesus teaches that it is not enough for us to love our neighbors who love us. We must love our enemies so that we may be children of our Father in heaven.

Year B

The Lesson   Isaiah 48:18–25
God speaks of his faithful care for his people Israel, though they have not responded to his love and forgiveness. "I am he who blots out your transgressions for my own sake, and I will not remember your sins."

Psalm 32 or 32:1–8
The psalmist thanks God for his forgiveness.

The Epistle   2 Corinthians 1:18–22
God is faithful and consistent. All the promises of God find the *"Yes!"* in Jesus Christ.

The Gospel   Mark 2:1–12
Four men lower a paralytic through a roof into Jesus' presence. Jesus speaks to the paralytic, "My son, your sins are forgiven." In Jesus' life on earth physical and mental illness were thought to be the result of sin and healing was related to forgiveness. Some of the scribes were in the room. They did not speak, but asked themselves, "How can this man forgive sins?" Jesus was aware of their unspoken questions. So that they

might know he had the authority to forgive sins, Jesus said to the paralytic, "I say to you, rise, take up your pallet and go home."

Year C

The Lesson   Genesis 45:3–11, 21–28

Joseph declares his identity to his brothers and asks if their father is still living. Joseph believes that all that happened to him at the hands of his brothers was God's will and that God sent him to Egypt to preserve life there. His brothers return to their father Jacob with Joseph's gifts, and Jacob says, "Joseph my son is still alive. I will go and see him before I die."

Psalm 37: 1–18 or 37:3–10

The psalmist counsels patience, though the wicked seem to prosper. The Lord will uphold the righteous.

The Epistle   1 Corinthians 15:35–38, 42–50

Further instruction to the people of the church at Corinth about resurrection after death. Paul explains that earthly bodies will be transformed into spiritual beings.

The Gospel   Luke 6:27–38

Jesus teaches: Love your enemies, do good to those who hate you, bless those who curse you, pray for those who abuse you. Do not judge and you will not be judged. Forgive, and you will be forgiven. The measure you give will be the measure you receive.

PROPER 3:

The Sunday closest to May 25
Themes of the Collect:

- We ask God to grant that the course of the world may be peaceably governed by his providence,
- and that his Church may joyfully serve him in confidence and security.

Year A

The Lesson   Isaiah 49:8–18

The prophet, speaking to the people of Israel in exile in Babylon, promises that God will comfort and redeem Israel; God will never forsake his people.

Psalm 62 or 62:6–14

All that is left to the psalmist is a total trust in God.

The Epistle   1 Corinthians 4:1–5 (6–7) 8–13

Paul describes in caustic terms his understanding of what it means to be Christ's servant. He describes his own life and that of Apollos as examples of service.

The Gospel   Matthew 6:24–34

Jesus urges his followers to trust in God to know their needs and to provide for them. Concern about material needs will draw them away from the fullness of life that God has promised.

Year B

The Lesson   Hosea 2:14–23

Israel is described by the prophet as a faithless wife whom God loves and will once more make his own. God will show his compassion, and the land will answer with grain, wine, and oil.

Psalm 103 or 103:1–6

A song of blessing to God for his grace and forgiveness.

The Epistle   2 Corinthians 3:(4–11) 17—4:2

Paul tells the congregation at Corinth that God is calling his servants to be ministers of a new covenant in the Spirit of the Lord that gives life.

The Gospel   Mark 2:18–22

Jesus answers the criticism that his followers do not fast by comparing his time with his disciples to the presence of the bridegroom at a marriage feast.

Year C

The Lesson Jeremiah 7:1–7 (8–15)

A warning sermon calls upon the people of Israel to change their lives. The people come to the temple and repeat devout phrases while they continue to live in oppressive and unjust ways.

Psalm 92 or 92:1–5, 11–14

A song of thanks, comparing the faithful and righteous to trees that flourish in the courts of the Lord.

The Epistle 1 Corinthians 15:50–58

Through our Lord Jesus Christ, God has given us victory over sin and death.

The Gospel Luke 6:39–49

Jesus teaches the meaning of discipleship, and asks, "Why do you call me 'Lord, Lord,' and not do what I tell you?" Those who hear his words and act on them are like people who build on foundations of rock. Those who hear and do not do Jesus' words are like those who build houses without foundations.

PROPER 4:

The Sunday closest to June 1
  Themes of the Collect:

- God's unfailing providence sets all things in heaven and earth in order.
- We pray that God will put all hurtful things away from us
- and that he will give us those things that are good and helpful for us.

Year A

The Lesson Deuteronomy 11:18–21, 26–28

Moses calls the people of Israel to obedience to God in the future. They are to take his words to heart and keep his commandments constantly before them if they want to live in the land that God promised to their forefathers. Moses offers them a choice between a blessing and a curse. The blessing will be theirs if they keep God's commands; the curse if they do not listen to the commandments of God but turn aside and follow gods they do not know.

Psalm 31 or 31:1–5, 19–24
  The psalmist commits himself to the Lord.

The Epistle Romans 3:21–25a, 28
  God's way of righting wrong depends upon the believer's faith and trust in Christ. All, both Jews and Gentiles, have sinned and fallen short of the glory of God. All are justified by God's free grace through the redemption that is in Jesus Christ. A person is justified by faith apart from success in keeping the law.

The Gospel Matthew 7:21–27
  False prophets follow Jesus and call him Lord; but only those who do the will of the Father will enter the Kingdom of heaven. The people who do God's will as well as talk about it are like those who build their houses on solid rock.

Year B

The Lesson Deuteronomy 5:6–21
  Moses calls the people of Israel together and gives them the Ten Commandments.

Psalm 81 or 81:1–10
  A song of praise for a festival, reminding the people that they may worship only the Lord their God.

The Epistle 2 Corinthians 4:5–12
  Paul writes that they are not proclaiming themselves, but Jesus Christ as Lord. God has caused his light to shine in them to reveal the glory of God through Christ. They ". . . have this treasure in earthen vessels . . ." to show that such power does not come from them; it is God's alone. Paul's sufferings permit him to share the death that Jesus died, and life that conquers death is present in him also.

The Gospel   Mark 2:23–28

Sabbath observance called for refraining from all work. When Jesus' disciples gathered grain in the fields, and he was asked why they were permitted to do what is forbidden on the Sabbath, Jesus replied that the Sabbath was made for man, not man for the Sabbath; and that the Son of Man is Lord even of the Sabbath.

Year C

The Lesson   I Kings 8:22–23, 27–30, 41–43

In the dedication ceremony, Solomon stood in front of the altar in the Temple he had just completed. He praised the Lord for keeping his promises. Solomon realizes that the Temple cannot contain God; but he prays that God will be present for the people who pray to him in the Temple, and also for people who come from far countries and pray to him, so that all the people of the earth may know that the Temple Solomon has built is called by God's name.

Psalm 96 or 96:1–9

Declare the glory of the Lord to all the nations.

The Epistle   Galatians 1:1–10

Paul writes to the Christian congregations of Galatia. He speaks of himself as an apostle independent of human authority, having been commissioned by God and Jesus Christ.

Paul is astonished to hear that the congregation in Galatia has turned away from the Gospel of Christ. He emphasizes that anyone who preaches a gospel at variance with the Gospel of Christ is to be considered an outcast.

The Gospel   Luke 7:1–10

A centurion in Capernaum had a valued servant who was dying. The centurion heard of Jesus, and sent a request that he would come and save the servant's life. When Jesus approached the house, the centurion sent a message to say that he knew that Jesus would not wish to enter the house of a non-Jew; but the centurion was sure that Jesus had only to say the word and his servant would be cured. Jesus said, "Nowhere, not even in Israel, have I found faith like this." When the messengers returned to the house the servant was in good health.

PROPER 5:

The Sunday closest to June 8

Year A
Themes of the Collect:

- All good comes from God.
- We ask that through God's inspiration our thoughts may be right
- and through God's guidance we may act on them.

The Lesson   Hosea 5:15—6:6
   God wants steadfast love and loyalty and not sacrifice; knowledge of God rather than burnt offerings. The qualities that preserve the covenant between God and his people go beyond ritual worship, so Israel's apparent remorse and repentance for the worship of other gods are unacceptable.

Psalm 50 or 50:7–15
   God has no need that can be satisfied by animal sacrifices. He asks that his people offer the sacrifice of thanksgiving and keep his moral laws.

The Epistle   Romans 4:13–18
   Faith, not law, was at the heart of God's promise to Abraham and his descendants. It is a matter of grace and it is valid not only for Abraham's descendants but for those who have the faith of Abraham.

The Gospel   Matthew 9:9–13
   Jesus calls Matthew, a tax gatherer, to follow him. Jesus' disciples were asked why their master ate with tax collectors and sinners. (Tax collectors were scorned as servants of the Roman occupation.) Jesus heard their question and replied that healthy people do not need doctors. He said he had not come to call righteous people, but sinners, to repentance. He suggested that they think about the words of Scripture: "I desire mercy, not sacrifice."

Year B

The Lesson   Genesis 3:(1–7) 8–21
   The disobedience of Adam and Eve in the Garden of Eden. The myth

suggests that the difficulties of life in the world are of people's own making rather than the kind of life God wished for his creation.

Psalm 130
A song of repentance, calling upon the Lord for his promised forgiveness.

The Epistle   2 Corinthians 4:13–18
We know that God who raised the Lord Jesus to life will raise us too. Our eyes are fixed on the things that are unseen; what is seen passes away; the unseen is eternal.

The Gospel   Mark 3:20–35
Jesus was confronted with accusations that the good he was doing came from Satan's power. Jesus told his accusers that we sin against the Holy Spirit when we do not see that Satan may be present in our judgments of others. Asked to come out to his mother and brothers, Jesus looked at the people in the circle round him and responded, ''Whoever does the will of God is my brother, my sister, my mother.''

Year C

The Lesson   1 Kings 17:17–24
The son of the mistress of the house where Elijah lived became ill and died. God heard Elijah's prayer and returned life to the child's body.

Psalm 30 or 30:1–6, 12–13
A hymn of praise and thanksgiving for recovery from sickness to health. ''You have put off my sackcloth and clothed me with joy.''

The Epistle   Galatians 1:11–24
Paul writes that the gospel he preaches comes from God, revealed by Jesus Christ, and not from any human agency. Paul recounts his own early history and his call to proclaim Christ among non-Jews.

The Gospel   Luke 7:11–17
With his disciples and a number of other people, Jesus went to a town called Nain where they met a funeral. Jesus' heart went out to the woman who had lost her only son, and he told her not to weep. When Jesus said, ''Young man, rise up!'' the man who had been dead sat up and spoke,

and Jesus gave him back to his mother. The people were filled with awe and said, "A great prophet has arisen among us," and "God has shown his care for his people."

PROPER 6:

The Sunday closest to June 15
  Themes of the Collect:

  • We ask that God will keep his household the Church firm in faith and love for him,
  • so that we may speak God's truth boldly
  • and give help and service justly and with compassion.

Year A

The Lesson Exodus 19:2–8a
  The people of Israel camped in the wilderness of Sinai, where the Lord called Moses and told him to tell the people that if they will listen to him and keep his covenant, of all the people of the earth they shall be God's special people, his kingdom of priests, his holy nation. When Moses gave God's message to the elders, they all answered together, "Whatever the Lord has said we will do."

Psalm 100
  We are God's people and the sheep of his pasture.

The Epistle Romans 5:6–11
  Christ died for us while we were sinners. Since we have been justified by Christ's death, we shall be saved by him from the Final Judgment. We rejoice in God through our Lord Jesus; through him we have been granted reconciliation.

The Gospel Matthew 9:35—10:8 (9–15)
  As Jesus went through the towns and villages, he was moved to pity by the needs of the people he saw. He said to his disciples that the harvest was plentiful, but that there were few workers to gather it; they should pray to the Lord to send laborers to gather the crop.
  The names of the twelve disciples are listed in the passage. They are given authority to cast out unclean spirits and to cure all sorts of sickness.

They are to go to ". . . the lost sheep of the house of Israel, preaching as they go that the Kingdom of heaven is at hand."

Year B

The Lesson   Ezekiel 31:1–6, 10–14

The Lord sent a message to Pharaoh by the prophet Ezekiel, saying that in its greatness Egypt was like Assyria, a splendid tree that had no rival in all the Garden of Eden. Because its pride mounted as it grew, the Lord made an example of it, and turned it over to strangers from the most ruthless of nations.

Psalm 92 or 92:1–4, 11–14

A psalm of thanksgiving comparing the righteous who are planted in the house of the Lord to palm trees and cedars of Lebanon, green and succulent even in old age.

The Epistle   2 Corinthians 5:1–10

Paul lives in the sure hope that our spirit bodies will be eternal, destined for life in heaven. Paul longs for the time to come when the change is complete and human suffering ended. Our lives will be laid open before Christ, and all will receive their due for their conduct in the body.

The Gospel   Mark 4:26–34

Jesus taught the people parables of the Kingdom of God; how seed, scattered on the land in secret, grows until it has produced a crop and harvest time has come; or the tiny mustard seed, which once planted grows taller and larger than other plants and forms branches to make shade for the birds.

Year C

The Lesson 2 Samuel 11:26—12:10, 13–15

The consequences of King David's adultery with Bathsheba. After Uriah died, when the period of her mourning was over, David brought Bathsheba to his home, where she bore a son. What David had done was wrong in the eyes of the Lord. The Lord sent Nathan to David with a rebuke and a prophecy. The child Bathsheba had borne would die.

Psalm 32 or 32:1–8
Thanksgiving for God's forgiveness.

The Epistle   Galatians 2:11–21
Paul argues with Cephas (Peter) over eating with Gentile Christians, saying that God's acceptance comes through faith rather than through observance of laws. If righteousness comes through law, Christ died for nothing.

The Gospel   Luke 7:36–50
Jesus eats dinner in a Pharisee's home, where a woman who was leading an immoral life in the town came and kissed Jesus' feet and wet them with her tears and dried them with her hair. Then she anointed them with myrrh. When the Pharisee criticized Jesus for permitting this, he pointed out the Pharisee's omissions of courtesies to a guest: no kiss of greeting, no oil for his head, no water for his feet. Jesus said to the woman, "Your sins are forgiven," and "Your faith has saved you. Go in peace."

PROPER 7:

The Sunday closest to June 22
Themes of the Collect:

- God never fails to help and direct the people he has placed upon the secure foundation of his loving-kindness.
- We pray that he will give us constant love and reverence for his Holy Name.

Year A

The Lesson   Jeremiah 20:7–13
Jeremiah prays out of his feeling that he has been badly treated by God. He would stop speaking in God's name but he cannot. God's word is like a fire blazing in his heart. He needs God on his side, and he cries to the Lord for vengeance against his persecutors.

Psalm 69:1–18 or 69:7–10, 16–18
The lament of a person deep in distress who calls upon the Lord to save him from his enemies.

The Epistle   Romans 5:15b–19

Paul contrasts Adam with Christ, sin with righteousness, disobedience with obedience, condemnation with acquittal, death for everyone with life through Jesus Christ for everyone.

The Gospel   Matthew 10:(16–23) 24–33

Jesus assures the disciples that they are of great value in the Father's eyes and that God knows what is happening to them. He tells them of the persecutors who will come to them for his sake; but they must witness to what they know. Those who kill the body cannot kill the soul.

Year B

The Lesson   Job 38:1–11, 16–18

The Lord answered Job out of the whirlwind, asking by what wisdom Job can question the Creator of everything in earth and in heaven, the Lord who controls the sea.

Psalm 107:1–32 or 107:1–3, 23–32

A thanksgiving for those delivered by God. "Some went down to the sea in ships."

The Epistle   2 Corinthians 5:14–21

God has reconciled us to him through Christ and entrusted us with the message of reconciliation, so we come as ambassadors for Christ. Christ accepted our sinfulness so that our misdeeds would no longer be held against us, so that in Christ we may be made one with the goodness of God.

The Gospel   Mark 4:35–41: (5:1–20)

When a storm came up on the lake and frightened the disciples, Jesus rebuked the wind and commanded the sea to be still. His followers were filled with awe and asked, "Who can this be? Even the wind and the sea obey him."

Year C

The Lesson   Zechariah 12:8–10; 13:1

A prophecy of the Lord's victory for the people of Jerusalem and the

House of David. He will give them a spirit of compassion, so that when they look on the one they have pierced, they will mourn.

Psalm 63:1–8
The psalmist is searching for God. He thirsts for God, and sings his praise.

The Epistle   Galatians 3:23–29
We were held prisoners of the law until Christ came to us. Baptized into union with Christ, there is no such thing as Jew or Greek, slave or free man, male or female—all are one in Christ Jesus.

The Gospel   Luke 9:18–24
Jesus asked his disciples, "Who do the people say that I am?" They replied, "Some say you are John the Baptist, and others Elijah, and others say that one of the old prophets has come to life." Jesus asked, "Who do you say that I am?" and Peter answered, "The Christ of God." Jesus ordered them not to tell this to anyone, and predicted his future sufferings. Jesus said, "Whoever cares for his own safety is lost, but if a person loses his life for my sake, he will be saved."

PROPER 8:

The Sunday closest to June 29
   Themes of the Collect:

- God has built his Church on the foundation of the apostles and prophets.
- Jesus Christ is the chief cornerstone of the Church.
- We ask God to grant that we may be brought together in unity of spirit by their teaching
- so that we may be a holy temple acceptable to God.

Year A

The Lesson   Isaiah 2:10–17
The prophet proclaims the Day of the Lord, which will bring the downfall of everything that is high and lifted up. "The pride of men shall be brought low; and the Lord alone will be exalted in that day."

Psalm 89:1–18 or 89:1–4, 15–18
A song of praise to the Creator, whose love is faithful and just.

The Epistle   Romans 6:3–11
When we were baptized into union with Christ, we were baptized into his death, and we believe that we shall also come to life with him. We must regard ourselves as dead to sin and alive to God in Christ Jesus.

The Gospel   Matthew 10:34–42
Jesus, speaking to his disciples, explained that proclamation of the Kingdom of God as a disciple of Jesus meant obedience and discipleship, and that discipleship came before everything else in life. Those who give up their lives for Jesus' sake will find life.

Year B

The Lesson   Deuteronomy 15:7–11
The reading is from the statutes and laws delivered to Moses by God, and follows a passage on the remission of debts which was to occur every seventh year. God commanded his people to be generous to one another and to lend as much as was needed. When requests for help came close to the seventh year, it was tempting to refuse because the debt might never be repaid. God warned that to refuse to help the poor was sin, and that he would bless the openhanded.

Psalm 112
Those who are in a right relationship with God and who are righteous, gracious, compassionate, and good in their dealings with others will be blessed by the Lord.

The Epistle   2 Corinthians 8:1–9, 13–15
Paul describes the generosity of the churches in Macedonia in giving to the offering for the poor of the churches in Jerusalem. God accepts what we have to give. The need in Jerusalem is great and Paul is trying to bring about a relationship of mutual responsibility among the churches.

The Gospel   Mark 5:22–24, 35b–43
Jairus, a leader in one of the synagogues, came to Jesus and begged

him to save the life of Jairus's daughter. While Jairus was pleading with Jesus, a messenger came to say that the child was dead. Jesus told Jairus not to be afraid but to have faith. He went to Jairus's house where many people were mourning. Except for the parents and his disciples he sent the others out of the room. Jesus took the girl's hand and said, "Get up, my child." The girl got up and walked about, and Jesus told her parents not to talk about what had happened; and to get their daughter something to eat.

Year C

The Lesson   1 Kings 19:15–16, 19–21
The Lord sends Elijah to anoint the kings of Syria and Israel, and to anoint Elisha to be prophet in Elijah's place. Elisha then follows Elijah.

Psalm 16 or 16:5–11
God's presence is joy and contentment.

The Epistle   Galatians 5:1, 13–25
Christ set us free, therefore we must not become slaves again. Freedom is not license. The harvest of the Spirit is love, joy, peace, patience, kindness, goodness, faithfulness, and self-control. There is no law against these. Paul urges Christians to walk by the Spirit without conceit or envy of one another.

The Gospel   Luke 9:51–62
Jesus and his friends were traveling to Jerusalem. They were refused accommodations in a Samaritan village because the Samaritans objected to worship in Jerusalem. James and John wanted to destroy the village; Jesus rebuked them, and they continued on their way.

People who wished to become followers of Jesus came to him, and each had a reason why he could not come now. Jesus told them that discipleship means putting the Kingdom of God ahead of every other responsibility or relationship.

PROPER 9:

The Sunday closest to July 6
   Themes of the Collect:

- God has taught us that all his commandments are kept if we love God and our neighbor.
- We ask that through the grace of the Holy Spirit we may love God with our whole hearts
- and be united to one another with pure affection.

Year A

The Lesson　Zechariah 9:9–12
The word of the Lord brings a prophecy of salvation for Jerusalem; her king is coming, his victory won, humbly, mounted on the foal of an ass. His rule shall extend to the ends of the earth.

Psalm 145 or 145:8–14
A hymn of praise for the goodness of God. His kingdom is everlasting.

The Epistle　Romans 7:21—8:6
Paul is divided, in his inmost self he knows that he delights in the law, but sin has power over him. He is still responsible for what he does. The Spirit of life in Christ Jesus has set Paul free from the law of sin and death.

The Gospel　Matthew 11:25–30
Jesus thanks God for his revelations and his trust. He calls all those whose work is hard and whose load is heavy to come to him and learn from his teachings; in them burdened souls will find relief.

Year B

The Lesson　Ezekiel 2:1–7
Ezekiel is called to be God's prophet to the people of Israel, a nation of rebels. Ezekiel is not to be afraid of them; he is to speak God's words to them whether they listen or not.

Psalm 123
A plea for help from God.

The Epistle　2 Corinthians 12:2–10
Paul had been granted visions and revelations. He speaks of the magnificence of the revelations, and of his own weakness. Paul realizes that his weakness is turned into strength through God's grace.

The Gospel   Mark 6:1–6

Jesus and his disciples went to Nazareth, his home; and on the Sabbath he taught in the synagogue. The people of the congregation were offended. They wondered how the carpenter, Mary's son, whose brothers and sisters lived in Nazareth, had so much wisdom and was able to work miracles. Jesus said that a prophet would be honored anywhere but in his native town among his family. He was dismayed by the lack of faith of the people of Nazareth.

Year C

The Lesson   Isaiah 66:10–16

God will come to bring peace and prosperity to his people and judgment to his enemies.

Psalm 66 or 66:1–8

A thanksgiving hymn—Let psalms declare the glory of God's name.

The Epistle   Galatians 6:(1–10) 14–18

Because circumcision would bring Christians under the protection of the Jewish law and they would escape persecution, pressure was brought to bear on uncircumcised Gentiles. Paul said that circumcision doesn't matter; all that matters is the new creation in Christ.

The Gospel   Luke 10:1–12, 16–20

Jesus chose seventy people to carry on the mission and sent them in pairs to the towns he would visit himself. He spoke to them of the demands of discipleship and how they should visit the people of the towns. The seventy were given the power to defeat the forces of evil and their names are written in heaven.

PROPER 10:

The Sunday closest to July 13

Themes of the Collect:

- We ask God to receive our prayers when we call upon him
- to grant that we may know and understand what we ought to do
- and to give us grace and power to do the things he directs faithfully.

Year A

The Lesson   Isaiah 55:1–5, 10–13

A poem to celebrate God's generosity, faithfulness, and power. All are invited to the Lord's table; those who listen will have life. God will make a covenant with Israel forever, and all the world will show forth God's power.

Psalm 65 or 65:9–14

A thanksgiving praising God for the wonderful things he does for the people of the earth.

The Epistle   Romans 8:9–17

Sin made us slaves; the Spirit of God makes us God's children. If we are God's children, then we are his heirs and fellow-heirs with Christ. If we share Christ's sufferings now, we may share his glory hereafter.

The Gospel   Matthew 13:1–9, 18–23

Jesus taught the crowds that gathered around him on the beach the parable of the sower and the seed, and its inner meaning.

Year B

The Lesson   Amos 7:7–15

The Lord showed Amos a vision of a man beside a wall with a plumb line (to make sure the wall was vertical and therefore strong) and told Amos that he was setting a plumb line to test his people Israel, and that he would rise against Jeroboam (the king of Israel). The priest of Bethel told Jeroboam that Amos was conspiring against him and prophesying his death, and told Amos to go away and never to prophesy again at Bethel. Amos said he was not a prophet; but the Lord had ordered him to go and prophesy to the people of Israel.

Psalm 85 or 85:7–13

A prayer for deliverance and peace.

The Epistle   Ephesians 1:1–14

Paul's letter to the church at Ephesus begins with a prayer of praise to God for all that he has done for us in Christ.

The Gospel   Mark 6:7–13

On a teaching journey through the villages, Jesus called the twelve and sent them out by twos on a mission. He gave them authority over evil spirits, told them what to take with them and what to leave at home, and how to carry on their work of preaching and healing. They preached that people should repent of their sins, and healed many who were sick.

Year C

The Lesson   Deuteronomy 30:9–14

Those who obey the Lord and keep his commandments will prosper in all that they do. The commandments which the Lord gives are not difficult or remote, they are very near, upon peoples' lips and in their hearts, ready to be kept.

Psalm 25 or 25:3–9

A prayer for guidance and help from the Lord.

The Epistle   Colossians 1:1–14

Paul's letter to "God's people at Colossae" is a prayer of hope that God will give them wisdom and insight into his will, and strength and power to meet whatever comes with patience and joy.

The Gospel   Luke 10:25–37

A lawyer who put a question to Jesus: "What must I do to inherit eternal life?" was answered with questions about how he read what was written in the law. He responded with the two great commandments— love for God and for neighbor. Jesus said if the lawyer kept those commandments he would live. The lawyer went on to ask, "Who is my neighbor?" and Jesus replied with the story of the good Samaritan. Jews of that day would have expected nothing good from a Samaritan, which sharpens the parable.

PROPER 11:

The Sunday closest to July 20
Themes of the Collect:

- God is the source of all wisdom.
- He knows what we need before we ask him.

- He understands that we often do not know what to ask.
- We pray that he will look on our weakness with compassion,
- and give us those things we dare not ask, because we do not feel worthy to receive them
- or because of our blindness, we cannot ask.

Year A

The Lesson   Wisdom 12:13, 16–19
God is the only God, the world is his, and he has no need to justify his decisions. He is a just and merciful God whose kindness to his children does not come from weakness. He has filled his children with hope by the offer of forgiveness for repentance for their sins.

Psalm 86 or 86:11–17
A prayer to the Lord, who has been the psalmist's help and comfort, for protection and rescue.

The Epistle   Romans 8:18–25
As we share in the sufferings of Christ, and wait for God to set us free, all of nature suffers with us. With the whole universe, we want to be set free from bondage to mortality and to receive the glorious freedom that is our heritage as children of God.

The Gospel   Matthew 13:24–30, 36–43
Jesus told his listeners another parable of the Kingdom of heaven; The story of the weeds in the wheat field and an interpretation of the parable, which was given to his disciples when they asked him its meaning.

Year B

The Lesson   Isaiah 57:14b–21
God reassures the contrite and humble and promises healing to them. But there is to be no peace for the wicked, who are like a troubled sea that cannot rest.

Psalm 22:22–30
A hymn of praise to the Lord who rules over the nations, yet listens to the humble and downtrodden.

The Epistle   Ephesians 2:11–22

The law of the Jewish people stood like a "dividing wall" between Jews and Gentiles. Paul reminds the congregation at Ephesus that Christ is our peace; and he has made the two one, annulling the law to make a single new humanity.

The Gospel   Mark 6:30–44

An account of the feeding of five thousand.

Year C

The Lesson   Genesis 18:1–10a (10b–14)

As Abraham was sitting at the opening of his tent, he looked up and saw three men standing before him. Abraham was a gracious host and hurried to provide refreshment and food for the men, and waited on them himself. The Bible tells us that the Lord said, "I will come back to you in the spring, and Sarah your wife shall have a son."

Abraham and Sarah were old, and Sarah had passed the age of childbearing. Sarah laughed to herself, because she thought what was promised was impossible. The Lord asked Abraham, "Why did Sarah laugh? Is anything too hard for the Lord? Sarah shall have a son."

Psalm 15

The psalm describes ten qualities of the life of a person who seeks to be worthy to worship the Lord.

The Epistle   Colossians 1:21–29

Paul writes of the reconciled community which must continue in the faith and hope of the gospel. The sufferings with which Paul is afflicted are to be endured for the sake of Christ's body, the Church.

The Gospel   Luke 10:38–42

Mary and Martha were sisters in whose home Jesus visited. Mary sat at Jesus' feet, listening to his teaching, while Martha was doing all tasks of preparation for guests. Martha protested and wanted Jesus to tell Mary to help her. Jesus answered, "Martha, Martha, you fret about so many things. Only one thing is necessary. Mary has chosen the best part and it shall not be taken away from her."

PROPER 12:

The Sunday closest to July 27
  Themes of the collect:

- God protects everyone who trusts in him,
- and without him nothing is strong, nothing is holy.
- We pray that his mercy to us may increase,
- and with God as our ruler and guide
- we may so live in this world
- that we do not lose the things that are eternal.

Year A

The Lesson   1 Kings 3:5–12
  The Lord God appeared to King Solomon in a dream and asked, "What shall I give you?" Solomon expressed his gratitude to God for the great and constant love he showed to Solomon's father, David. Solomon felt very young and unprepared for the responsibilities that had come to him, and he asked the Lord to give him an understanding mind so that he might govern his people well, and distinguish between good and evil. The Lord was pleased by Solomon's request, and said that because Solomon had not asked for long life or riches or the lives of his enemies, God would give him a heart so wise and understanding that there never had been or would be a king like him.

Psalm 119:121–136 or 119:129–136
  The psalmist prays for insight to understand the instruction of the Lord.

The Epistle   Romans 8:26–34
  Through the Spirit's intercession, God's love and care support us in our weakness. God's purpose is for us to be like his Son. It is Christ who is at God's right hand, who intercedes for us.

The Gospel   Matthew 13:21–22, 44–49a
  The gospel reading is made up of five short parables. Jesus taught that the Kingdom of heaven is like

The Season After Pentecost   *193*

- a mustard seed, tinier than any other seed. When the seed has grown it becomes a tree big enough for birds to rest in.
- yeast, which a woman mixed with half a hundredweight of flour until it was all leavened.
- a treasure buried in a field. The finder buried it again and sold everything he had to buy the field.
- a fine pearl of great value. The merchant sold everything he had and bought it.
- a net placed in the sea in which all kinds of fish are caught. The fishermen brought the net ashore and put the good fish into pails and threw away the worthless ones.

Year B

The Lesson   2 Kings 2:1–15

The time had come when the Lord would take Elijah to heaven. Three times Elijah told Elisha to stay while Elijah went on to a place where the Lord had sent him, and each time Elisha said, "I will not leave you."

Elijah and Elisha came together to the Jordan followed by fifty prophets. Elijah rolled up his mantle and struck the water with it. The water parted and they crossed on dry ground. Elijah asked "What can I do for you before I am taken from you?" Elisha said, " . . . let me inherit a double share of your spirit." Elijah said that could only happen if Elisha saw Elijah as he was taken away. A chariot and horses of fire came between them and Elijah vanished in a whirlwind.

Elisha tore his clothes in mourning, and picked up Elijah's mantle, crying to the Lord as he struck the water with it. The water divided and Elisha crossed to where the prophets were waiting. They met him, bowing low, saying, "The spirit of Elijah rests on Elisha."

Psalm 114

A song of thanksgiving, praising God who saved the people of Israel in the Exodus.

The Epistle   Ephesians 4:1–7, 11–16

Paul, writing to the Christians at Ephesus, calls them to be humble, patient, and loving toward one another. The variety of individual gifts which equip God's people for their mission in his service contributes to the unity of the Church.

The Gospel   Mark 6:45–52

Jesus walks on the water. When Jesus had fed the thousands of people he sent his disciples to the other side of the lake in the boat. When the crowds had left, Jesus went into the hills to pray alone. After midnight Jesus came down from the hills and walked across the lake to meet the boat. When the disciples saw him walking on the water they were frightened, and cried, "It is a ghost!" Jesus called to them not to be afraid. He climbed into the boat and the wind dropped. The disciples were dumbfounded, they had not understood what had happened with the loaves and fishes.

(See Matthew 14:13–21; John 6:1–13)

Year C

The Lesson   Genesis 18:20–33

Abraham pleads for Sodom. God told Abraham that the wickedness in Sodom and Gomorrah was very great. Abraham asked God, "Are you really going to destroy the good people with the sinners? There might be fifty good men in the town. Will you not spare the town for the sake of the good men to see that justice is done?" God replied that he would spare the whole town if there were fifty good men. Abraham continues his pleading until God agreed to spare Sodom if there were only ten good men. The Lord cares about individuals and in his judgment shows mercy.

Psalm 138

A song of thanksgiving to the Lord, who answers prayer and cares for his people.

The Epistle   Colossians 2:6–15

Paul warns the congregation at Colossae against false teaching, and tells them to be rooted in Christ, firm in the faith they have been taught, and to let their hearts overflow with thankfulness for what God has done for us in Christ Jesus.

The Gospel   Luke 11:1–13

Jesus teaches his disciples to pray and tells them to ask, and they will receive; to knock, and the door will be opened to them. If they, who are sinful human beings, know how to give their children good gifts, how much more will their heavenly Father give the Holy Spirit to those who ask?

The Sunday closest to August 3
  Themes of the Collect:

- We pray that God's continual mercy may cleanse and defend the Church;
- and because the Church cannot continue in safety without God's help
- we ask that he will always protect and govern it by his goodness.

Year A

The Lesson Nehemiah 9:16–20
  The scribe Ezra reviews the faithfulness and compassion of God toward the people of Israel during the Exodus, even when they were arrogant, stubborn, and disobedient. He fed them in the wilderness.

Psalm 78:1–29 or 78:14–20, 23–25
  The psalmist teaches events from the history of the people of Israel and the wonderful acts of God in their behalf. "He rained down manna upon them."

The Epistle Romans 8:35–39
  Paul is convinced that neither "death nor life, nor angels nor principalities, nor things present nor things to come, nor powers, nor height nor depth, nor anything else in all creation will be able to separate us from the love of God in Christ Jesus our Lord."

The Gospel Matthew 14:13–21
  Jesus feeds five thousand people. Jesus had been trying to find a quiet place for his disciples and himself; but everywhere he went people followed, and when he stepped out of the boat there was a great crowd waiting for him. He healed the sick in the crowd, and taught the people until it grew late and the disciples suggested he send the people away to buy food for themselves. "They need not go away," Jesus said. "You

196   A Summary of the Lectionary Texts

give them something to eat.'' ''We have only five barley loaves and two fish,'' the disciples replied. Jesus asked that these be brought to him and told the crowd to sit on the grass. Jesus blessed and broke the loaves and the disciples gave them to the people. All ate and were satisfied; and there were twelve baskets of food left over.

Year B

The Lesson   Exodus 16:2–4, 9–15
God provides food in the desert. The people of Israel complained about Moses and Aaron, and wished they had never left Egypt where at least they had food. The Lord said to Moses, ''I have heard the murmurings of the people. Tell them that at twilight they shall eat flesh and in the morning have their fill of bread so that they may know I am the Lord your God.'' In the morning quails came, and there was a fine stuff like flakes of frost on the ground. The people asked what it was, and Moses replied, ''It is the bread the Lord has given you to eat.''

Psalm 78:1–25 or 78:14–20, 23–25
See the Psalm, Year A.

The Epistle   Ephesians 4:17–25
Christians must be made new in mind and spirit. They must throw off falsehood and speak the truth to one another because we are all parts of the same body.

The Gospel   John 6:24–35
The crowd that had received the loaves and fishes searched for Jesus and found him. He said he knew they had come because they had eaten and satisfied their hunger; but that they must work for the food that lasts, the food of eternal life, which he would give them because God the Father had set the seal of his authority upon him. The people asked what they must do, to be doing the works of God, and Jesus said that what God requires is that they must believe in the one he has sent.

They asked for a sign so they might believe him. Their ancestors were given manna to eat in the desert. Jesus replied that it was not Moses who gave their forebears the bread from heaven, but God, who gives the real bread that brings life to the world. They asked him to give them real bread now and always; and Jesus answered, ''I am the bread of life. Whoever comes to me shall never be hungry or thirsty.''

Year C

The Lesson   Ecclesiastes 1:12–14; 2:(1–7, 11) 18–23
A deeply pessimistic view of life seeing everything we do as foolishness, emptiness, and chasing after wind. We toil all our lives and die and leave the fruits of our labor to those who come after us who have done nothing to deserve our hard work. A person's days are full of pain, work is a vexation, and even in the night his mind does not rest.

Psalm 49 or 49:1–11
The psalmist teaches that life is short, and that all people, rich or poor, wise or foolish, must die.

The Epistle   Colossians 3:(5–11) 12–17
Christians must give up their old natures completely and be the people God has chosen—kind, humble, gentle, patient. Whatever is done is to be done in the name of the Lord Jesus, giving thanks to God the Father through him.

The Gospel   Luke 12:13–21
Jesus refuses to be judge in the division of a family property. He told a parable of a man who gathered wealth for himself, but was a pauper in the sight of God.

PROPER 14:

The Sunday closest to August 10
Themes of the Collect:

- We ask that God will give us the spirit to think and do the things that are right.
- We cannot exist without God
- and we pray that he will enable us to live according to his will.

Year A

The Lesson   Jonah 2:1–9
Jonah prayed to the Lord his God from the belly of the great fish, and his prayer reads like a psalm. Jonah describes the sensations of drowning, and ends by saying that he will keep his vows, victory is the Lord's.

Psalm 29

The psalmist describes God as a tremendous thunderstorm, echoing over the waters, splintering the cedars of Lebanon, and making the wilderness writhe in pain.

The Epistle   Romans 9:1–5

Paul expresses his great grief at Israel's unbelief in Jesus Christ. The people of Israel were made God's sons; they had the covenants, the law, the worship in the temple, and God's promises. The patriarchs were part of their history, and the Messiah himself came from their roots.

The Gospel   Matthew 14:22–33

Jesus walks on the water. After Jesus had fed the crowds of people with the loaves of bread and the fish, he sent the disciples to the other side of the lake. When the people had gone, Jesus went up on the hillside to pray. Between three and six o'clock he walked across the water to the boat. The disciples were terrified, but Jesus reassured them.

Peter called, "Lord, if it is you, tell me to come to you over the water." "Come," said Jesus. Peter left the boat and walked toward Jesus. When Peter felt the strength of the wind he was frightened and began to sink. He called to Jesus, "Save me, Lord!" Jesus reached out and held Peter and asked, "Why did you doubt?" They climbed into the boat and the wind stopped. The disciples in the boat knelt before Jesus, crying, "Truly you are the Son of God."

Year B

The Lesson   Deuteronomy 8:1–10

Moses reminded the people of Israel of all that God had done for them during their forty years in the wilderness. The road by which God had led them was to discipline them; and they must keep his commandments. God fed them on manna which no one had eaten before, to teach them that people do not live by bread alone, but by every word that comes from God. Now God is bringing them to a rich land where they will have plenty to eat, and they will bless God for the rich land he has given them.

Psalm 34 or 34:1–8

A song of thanksgiving for the deliverance of the Lord. The psalmist invites all to "taste and see that the Lord is good."

The Epistle   Ephesians 4: (25–29) 30—5:2
Paul explains that falsehood, anger, dishonesty, and bad language
have no part in the life of a Christian. He urges the congregation at
Ephesus not to grieve the Holy Spirit, the seal with which we are marked
in our baptism, but to be generous, tenderhearted, and forgiving. As
God's dear children, they are to try to be like him and to live in love as
Christ loved them.

The Gospel   John 6:37–51
Jesus tells his listeners that he is the living bread which has come
down from heaven; those who eat this bread will live forever. The bread
Jesus gives is his own flesh and he gives it for the life of the world.

Year C

The Lesson   Genesis 15:1–6
Abram had a vision in which the Lord promised him a very great
reward. Abram wondered what the Lord could give him, since he had
not given him children, and Abram's heir was a slave. The Lord said
that Abram's heir would be his own son, and that Abram should look
into the sky and count the stars if he could. Abram would have as many
descendants as there were stars in the sky. Abram believed the Lord,
who counted his faith as righteousness.

Psalm 33 or 33:12–15, 18–22
The Lord looks with compassion on those who trust him.

The Epistle   Hebrews 11:1–3 (4–7) 8–16
The writer of the letter to the Hebrews calls the followers of Christ to
faith and describes faith as that which gives assurance to our hopes and
convinces us of realities we do not see.

The Gospel   Luke 12:32–40
Jesus tells his little community of followers that their Father in heaven
has chosen to give them the Kingdom. Therefore, they can trust themselves wholly to God. They are to hold themselves ready, because the
Son of Man will come when they least expect him.

PROPER 15:

The Sunday closest to August 17
   Themes of the Collect:

- God has given his only Son to be a sacrifice for our sin
- and an example of godly life.
- We ask God to give us grace to receive with thanks the fruits of our Lord's redeeming work,
- and to follow in the blessed steps of his holy life every day.

Year A

The Lesson   Isaiah 56:1 (2–5) 6–7
   The Lord calls his people to be just and to do right because deliverance is at hand. Foreigners who have given allegiance to the Lord are welcomed and encouraged to obey the laws. Their offerings and sacrifices shall be acceptable on God's altar; and his house shall be called a house of prayer for all nations.

Psalm 67
   A hymn of praise, asking the Lord to be gracious to us and bless us and to make his face shine upon us, that his saving power may be known among all nations.

The Epistle   Romans 11:13–15, 29–32
   Paul speaks as a missionary to the Gentiles, still seeking to save some of his own fellow Jews. If their rejection of Jesus Christ meant the reconciliation of the world, their acceptance of him would be like life from the dead.

The Gospel   Matthew 15:21–28
   A woman who was not Jewish came to Jesus, crying, ''Have pity on me! My daughter is tormented by a demon.'' Jesus did not reply, and his disciples urged him to send the woman away. Jesus said, ''I was sent only to the lost sheep of the house of Israel.'' The woman knelt at his feet and begged for help. Jesus said to her, ''It is not right to take the

children's bread and throw it to the dogs." "Yes, Lord," the woman answered, "yet even the dogs eat the scraps that fall from their master's table." Jesus said, "What faith you have! Let it be as you wish," and her daughter was restored to health from that moment.

Year B

The Lesson   Proverbs 9:1–6
In Proverbs and elsewhere in the Scriptures, Wisdom is represented as a person at God's side when he created the universe. Here she is like a gracious hostess who invites people to her dining table, promising those who accept that they will live and grow in understanding.

Psalm 147
A song of praise for God's might and power and for his special care of Israel.

or Psalm 34:9–14

The Epistle   Ephesians 5:15–20
Paul cautions the congregations to try to discern the will of the Lord and to act like sensible people. They are to let the Holy Spirit fill them and to give daily thanks for everything to God in the Lord Jesus Christ's name.

The Gospel   John 6:53–59
Jesus describes the central significance of the Eucharist—he is truly the bread of heaven, and whoever eats his flesh and drinks his blood shall receive eternal life.

Year C

The Lesson   Jeremiah 23:23–29
The writer speaks the word of the Lord: The Lord is the God who fills heaven and earth; he hears the lies of the self-appointed prophets who present their dreams as true prophecies and lead the people astray with their fantasies. They do not understand the power of God's word.

Psalm 82

God's judgment in heaven upon the unjust rulers who have failed the weak and the poor. The psalmist calls upon God to judge the earth.

The Epistle   Hebrews 12:1–7 (8–10) 11–14

The writer describes the Lord's discipline: He corrects his children; if he does not discipline us, we are not truly his children. Discipline seems painful, but in the end it gives those who have been trained in it the harvest of a worthy life. He urges his readers to seek to live at peace with all, and to lead a holy life, for without that no one will see the Lord.

The Gospel   Luke 12:49–56

Jesus says that he has come to bring the fire of judgment to the earth. He knows that martyrdom lies ahead for him. Before there can be peace there will be divisions, even among the members of families. People who know so well how to read the weather in the sky should be able to see the coming of the Kingdom in Jesus' presence on earth.

PROPER 16:

The Sunday closest to August 24
   Themes of the Collect:

- God's Chuch is gathered together in unity by his Holy Spirit.
- We pray that the Church may show forth his power among all peoples.

Year A

The Lesson   Isaiah 51:1–6

The Lord who kept his promises to Abraham and Sarah will restore Israel and bring deliverance to all the nations who look to the Lord for protection.

Psalm 138

A song of thanksgiving, praising the Lord who will accomplish his purpose for the psalmist, and whose love is forever.

The Epistle Romans 11:33–36

Paul praises the riches and wisdom and knowledge of God. Everything moves from him and through him and to him; and to him shall be glory forever.

The Gospel Matthew 16:13–20

Jesus' disciples tell him that some people are saying that he is John the Baptist, others that he is Elijah or Jeremiah or one of the prophets. Jesus asked, "Who do you say that I am?" Simon Peter answered, "You are the Messiah, the Son of the living God." Jesus said, "Simon, you did not learn that from any earthly source; it was revealed to you by my Father in heaven. And I tell you, you are Peter (the Rock) and on this rock I will build my Church, and the powers of death shall not conquer it. I will give you the keys of the Kingdom of Heaven; what you forbid on earth shall be forbidden in heaven and what you allow on earth shall be allowed in heaven." Jesus gave his disciples strict orders to tell no one that he was the Messiah.

Year B

The Lesson Joshua 24:1–2a, 14–25

Joshua brought all the tribes of Israel together at Shechem, saying to all the people, "This is the word of the Lord, the God of Israel: Serve the Lord in sincerity and with faithfulness. Cast away the gods your fathers worshiped in Egypt and serve the Lord. If you are unwilling to serve the Lord, choose this day whom you will serve; as for me and my house, we will serve the Lord." The people said they would serve the Lord, and Joshua called upon them to witness their decision. The people said, "The Lord our God we will serve, and his voice we will obey." Joshua made a covenant with the people that day at Shechem.

Psalm 16

Those who seek other gods than the Lord will find endless trouble; the psalmist blesses the Lord who has given him counsel and wisdom.

or 34:15–22

The Epistle Ephesians 5:21–33

Paul writes about the Christian life and the marriage relationship: "A man shall leave his father and mother and shall be joined to his wife, and the two shall become one flesh.''

The Gospel   John 6:60–69

Jesus heard his followers' shocked comments about what he had just told them: ''Whoever eats my flesh and drinks my blood has eternal life.'' Jesus was speaking of the bread of heaven, and of the life of the spirit; but many of his hearers were taking what he said literally. A number of those who had followed him had left him; and Jesus asked the Twelve if they also wanted to go. Peter answered him: ''You have the words of eternal life, and we believe and have come to know that you are the Holy One of God.''

Year C

The Lesson   Isaiah 28:14–22

The prophet warns the people of Israel about the treaty they have made with the forces of evil and death. The treaty will not save them; the Lord God has decreed destruction upon the whole land.

Psalm 46

God will show his mighty power in his final judgment of the world.

The Epistle   Hebrews 12:18–19, 22–29

Christians must remember that they stand in the light of the new covenant and not in the blazing fire of the old covenant. Christ's blood means reconciliation and forgiveness and not revenge. The new covenant makes possible the true worship of God.

The Gospel   Luke 13:22–30

Having known Jesus in his earthly life will not ensure participation in the Kingdom of God. People will come from everywhere for the feast; and some will expect to be included and will be shut out; while some who are now last shall be first.

PROPER 17:

The Sunday closest to August 31
   Themes of the Collect:

- God is the Lord of all power and might,
- the source and giver of all good things.
- We ask that he will enable the love of his Name to grow in our hearts,
- true religion to increase in our lives,
- that he will nourish us with all goodness,
- and bring forth in us the fruit of good works.

Year A

The Lesson   Jeremiah 15:15–21

Jeremiah argues his case to God like a person on trial, and says that God is treating him unfairly, like a brook whose waters fail in the dry season. The Lord answered Jeremiah: He has been running away, he must turn back to God. God is with Jeremiah to deliver and save him.

Psalm 26 or 26:1–8

The psalmist protests that his life has been an example to others; and he cries to the Lord for justice.

The Epistle   Romans 12:1–8

Paul appeals to the members of the Christian congregation in Rome to offer themselves to God as living sacrifices, in worship offered by mind and heart. They are no longer to follow the patterns of the world, but to let their whole beings be transformed. The gifts they have been given come from God's grace, and they must be used accordingly.

The Gospel   Matthew 16:21–27

Jesus began to explain his coming suffering and death to his disciples. Peter held his arm and said, "Lord, this shall never happen to you." Jesus tells Peter that he is thinking as people think and not as God thinks. Jesus' way is the way of the cross. Anyone who wishes to be a follower of Jesus must take up his cross and go with him.

Year B

The Lesson   Deuteronomy 4:1–9

Moses explains the importance of the laws to the people of Israel. If they obey the laws they will live in the land God will give them. They must not add nor take away anything from the law; but must carry out all the commandments of the Lord their God.

Psalm 15
The psalmist describes the person whose life makes him worthy to worship the Lord.

The Epistle   Ephesians 6:10–20
The writer describes the armor that is given to Christians by God so that they will be able to resist the powers of evil.

The Gospel   Mark 7:1–8, 14–15, 21–23
The Pharisees and scribes asked Jesus why his disciples did not live in accordance with tradition, but ate without washing their hands. Jesus said to those who were listening that it is not what goes into people that makes them unclean, it is the evil which comes out of their hearts that defiles them.

Year C

The Lesson   Ecclesiasticus 10:(7–11) 12–18
A poem on arrogance and pride, which are hateful to the Lord and to people.

Psalm 112
A song of praise to the Lord, describing a blessed generation of good people who live with confidence.

The Epistle   Hebrews 13:1–8
Christians are urged to love their fellow Christians; to show hospitality; to remember those in prison or those who are being mistreated; to keep the marriage bond intact; to be content with what they have; to honor their leaders and teachers and to follow their examples; and to remember that Jesus Christ is the same yesterday, today, and forever.

The Gospel   Luke 14:1, 7–14
Jesus tells a parable that illustrates humility: "For everyone who exalts himself will be humbled, and he who humbles himself shall be exalted." He also told his host, "When you give a feast, invite the poor,

the maimed, the lame, the blind; and you will be blessed, because they cannot repay you.''

The Sunday closest to September 7
   Themes of the Collect:

   • We ask God to grant us complete trust in him.
   • God resists those who are proud and certain of their own stength.
   • He never forsakes those who trust in his mercy for their security.

Year A

The Lesson   Ezekiel 33:(1–6) 7–11
   The Lord has appointed Ezekiel as a watchman for the people of Israel, to carry God's warnings to them. The Lord says that he does not desire the death of the wicked; but that they should turn away from evil and live.

Psalm 119:33–48 or 119:33–40
   The psalmist asks the Lord to teach him his ways and his laws and help him to keep God's commandments.

The Epistle   Romans 12:9–21
   A letter from Paul on the power of love. He counsels that so far as possible people should live at peace with one another, and not seek revenge. ''Vengeance is mine,'' says the Lord, ''I will repay.''

The Gospel   Matthew 18:15–20
   Jesus describes the ways in which the disciples are to respond if a member of the community commits a sin; he assures them that where two or three have come together in his Name he will be in the midst of them.

Year B

The Lesson   Isaiah 35:4–7a
   A poetic description of the return from exile. God comes to save those

to whom the captivity has seemed very long. "The eyes of the blind shall be opened, and the ears of the deaf unstopped."

Psalm 146 or146:4–9
A song of praise for God's great goodness to the poor and the oppressed.

The Epistle   James 1:17–27
Every perfect gift comes from the Father who never changes. We are to listen and be slow to anger, to put away everything that is unworthy, and accept the word that is planted in our hearts, which alone brings salvation. We are to be doers of the word, not only hearers.

The Gospel   Mark 7:31–37
A man who was deaf, who also had a speech impediment, was brought to Jesus to be healed. Jesus led the man away from the crowd, put his fingers into the man's ears, spat, and touched the man's tongue. Jesus spoke an Aramaic word that means "Be opened." The man's ears were opened and his speech was clear. Jesus asked the people who saw the healing not to tell anyone, but in their amazement they told it everywhere.

Year C

The Lesson   Deuteronomy 30:15–20
Moses offered the people of Israel a choice between life and good or death and evil. If they kept God's commandments they would live, their numbers would increase, and the Lord would bless them; if their hearts turned away from God they would perish. Moses told them, "I have set before you life and death, blessing and curse, therefore choose life . . ."

Psalm 1
The psalmist contrasts the ways of life open to people—good and evil, and their consequences, contentment and misery.

The Epistle   Philemon 1–20
Paul's plea for a runaway slave, Onesimus. Paul asks Philemon to receive Onesimus without punishment (penalties for recaptured slaves

were severe) and reminds Philemon that since Onesimus has become a Christian they are now brothers in Christ.

The Gospel   Luke 14:25–33
   On one occasion Jesus turned to the crowds that were following him and described the cost of discipleship. No one who does not put Jesus' work ahead of everything, even ahead of his own life, can be his disciple. No one can be his disciple without giving up all that he has.

PROPER 19:

The Sunday closest to September 14
   Themes of the Collect:

   • Without God we are unable to please him.
   • We ask that God's holy Spirit may direct our lives and rule our hearts in all things.

Year A

The Lesson   Ecclesiasticus 27:30—28:7
   Before people can expect mercy and forgiveness from the Lord, they must forgive their neighbors any offenses against them.

Psalm 103 or 103:8–13
   The Lord forgives and cares for his children.

The Epistle   Romans 14:5–12
   Paul reminds the people of the church in Rome that a loving person will respect the scruples of others. Whether we live or die, we belong to the Lord, and all of us will give accounts of ourselves to God.

The Gospel   Matthew 18:21–35
   Peter asked Jesus how often he must forgive his brother if his brother continued to wrong him. Jesus said that forgiveness has no limit, and he told the story of a man who had received great mercy from his master who forgave him a large debt. The man showed no forgiveness to those who were in debt to him. His master was very angry with him and threw him into prison until his debt was paid.

Year B

The Lesson   Isaiah 50:4–9

In the third of the servant songs in Isaiah, the servant tells about his work and his suffering. He knows the Lord will help him.

Psalm 116 or 116:1–8

A song of thanksgiving for deliverance from death.

The Epistle   James 2:1–5, 8–10, 14–18

No special treatment is to be given to the rich; the law to be observed is given in Scripture: "Love your neighbor as yourself." If faith only means believing in God, it is as lacking in life as wishing the needy good luck and doing nothing to help them. Faith that does not lead to action has no life.

The Gospel   Mark 8:27–38

In response to a question from Jesus, Peter answered that Jesus was the Messiah. Jesus ordered his disciples not to tell that to anyone, and began to speak plainly to his disciples about his coming sufferings, rejection, and death. Peter protested; and Jesus called Peter Satan because he was a tempter, seeking to draw Jesus from the agonies in store for him. Jesus said to all the people who were present, "Anyone who wants to be my follower must take up his cross and come with me."

or Mark 9:14–29

Year C

The Lesson   Exodus 32:1, 7–14

The people of Israel were tired of waiting for Moses to come down from the mountain and asked Aaron to make a god for them to worship. God was angry that the people should do such a disgraceful thing and said he would put an end to the people. Moses interceded, and the Lord relented and spared the people from the evil with which he threatened them.

Psalm 51:1–18 or 51:1–11

A lament, confessing sin and praying for forgiveness and renewal.

The Epistle   1 Timothy 1:12–17

Paul thanks God for judging him as trustworthy in spite of his persecution of God's people in former days. Paul feels that the grace of the
Lord has been given to him.

The Gospel   Luke 15:1–10

When the tax gatherers and people who were considered evil came to
hear Jesus, the learned people complained that Jesus welcomed sinners
and even ate with them. Jesus told two parables, in each of which there
is rejoicing over something that had been lost and was found again.

PROPER 20:

Sunday closest to September 21
Themes of the Collect:

- We ask God to grant us freedom from anxiety about earthly things
  and to love heavenly things;
- so that now, while we live among things that are passing away,
- we pray that we may hold fast to the things that will endure.

Year A

The Lesson   Jonah 3:10—4:11

The Lord sent Jonah to Ninevah to tell the people that the city would
be overthrown. The people believed the word of the Lord and ordered a
fast; and all the people, even the king, dressed in sackcloth. God saw
their repentance and did not destroy them.

Jonah was deeply angry about his success in turning the people of
Ninevah back to the Lord. The Lord recognized Jonah's anger and when
Jonah sat waiting, the Lord ordained a plant to grow and shade Jonah
from the heat. Jonah was grateful for the plant, but next day the Lord
ordained a worm to attack the plant and the plant withered. Jonah was
faint from the heat of the sun and prayed to die. God asked him, ''Are
you so angry over the plant?'' Jonah answered, ''Angry enough to die.''
The Lord said, ''You are sorry for the plant, though you did not tend it.
Should I not pity Ninevah, a great city with thousands of people?''

Psalm 145 or 145:1–8
A song of praise and blessing, expressing thanks for the Lord's goodness and compassion.

The Epistle   Philippians 1:21–27
Paul writes to the church at Philippi, saying that for him to live is Christ, and death is a gain because it will bring him closer to Christ; but he knows he still has work he must do. He wants to be sure that the Christians at Philippi are firm in the faith.

The Gospel   Matthew 20:1–16
Jesus tells his disciples a parable of the Kingdom of heaven, describing it as being like a landowner who hired laborers for his vineyard and paid all the workers the same wage, even if they had worked only during the hour before sunset. God's way of rewarding people does not conform to human standards. God said, ". . . and the last will be first, and the first last."

Year B

The Lesson   Wisdom 1:16—2:1 (6–11) 12–22
There were godless men who said to themselves that their lives were short and full of trouble with nothing to look forward to but death. They would take care to miss none of the good things in life because consequences didn't matter. They would tread poor and honest persons under foot. It doesn't matter about just persons, if they are children of God, God will save them, so they can be condemned to shameful death. Blinded by their own evil natures these men did not expect that holiness would have its reward, and they did not know the secret purposes of God.

Psalm 54
A prayer for help in trouble, asking for the downfall of enemies.

The Epistle   James 3:16—4:6
True wisdom is peace-loving, considerate, and reasonable. Jealousy and ambition bring disorder and evil. People want what they cannot have and pray for the wrong reasons. Scripture tells us, "God opposes the arrogant and gives grace to the humble."

The Gospel   Mark 9:30–37

Jesus was with his disciples, telling them of his coming suffering. They did not understand what he was saying, and later he asked them, "What were you talking about on the way?" They didn't want to tell him because they had been arguing about which of them was the greatest. Jesus called them around him and said, "If anyone wants to be first, he must make himself last, and be the servant of all." Jesus put his arm around a child and told them: "Anyone who receives a child like this in my name receives me; and whoever receives me, receives not me but him who sent me."

Year C

The Lesson   Amos 8:4–7 (8–12)

The prophet issues a warning to those who trample upon the poor and needy, who can't wait until the festivals are over to sell, so they can give short measure to the poor, "buy the poor for silver and the destitute for a pair of shoes." The Lord will never forget their doings.

Psalm 138

A wholehearted thanksgiving, praising the Lord who cares for the lowly.

The Epistle   1 Timothy 2:1–8

Paul urges that prayers be offered for all persons and for all in high office. It is God's will that all men should find salvation and come to know the truth.

The Gospel   Luke 16:1–13

Jesus told his disciples the story of a rich man who had a steward who was discharged for bad management of his master's property. The steward went to all the people who owed money to his master and settled their accounts by reducing the totals for immediate payment; and his master commended the steward for his action. Jesus' disciples must be able to act when need arises, and must know the uses of wealth, but never be enslaved by it.

The Sunday closest to September 28
  Themes of the Collect:

- God declares his almighty power chiefly in showing mercy and pity.
- We ask that he will grant us the completeness of his grace
- so that we, as we receive his promises,
- may share his heavenly treasure.

Year A

The Lesson   Ezekiel 18:1–4, 25–32
  The Lord disowns a proverb that came from long-ago teaching: "The fathers have eaten sour grapes, and the children's teeth are set on edge." When a person does what is just and right in all his relations with the Lord, he is freed from his parents' past and even from his own past. The prophet urges his hearers to get themselves new hearts and new spirits, and so live.

Psalm 25:1–14 or 25:3–9
  The psalmist prays for God's guidance and help.

The Epistle   Philippians 2:1–13
  Paul encourages humility and obedience in the members of the congregation at Philippi; and describes the humility of Jesus Christ in the words of an ancient hymn that extols the saving work of Christ. Paul counsels reverence, as they work out their salvation, for it is God who works in them for his purposes.

The Gospel   Matthew 21:28–32
  In a conversation in which the chief priests and elders were asking Jesus about the authority of John the Baptist, Jesus told a parable of a man who had two sons. The man told the first to go and work in the vineyard. The son replied that he would not, but later was sorry and went to the vineyard and did as his father asked. The father gave his other son the same order, and the son said he'd go at once, but never went.

"Which of the two did what his father asked?" Jesus inquired. They answered, "The first."

Jesus said, "Tax collectors and women of the streets (religious outcasts) are making their way into the Kingdom of God ahead of you. John came to show you how to live and you didn't believe him. These wretched outcasts believed him, and even when you saw that, you would not change your minds and believe him."

Year B

The Lesson Numbers 11:4–6, 10–16, 24–29

When the people of Israel were in the wilderness, new complaints and dissatisfaction came out at every difficulty. Moses spoke with the Lord and told him that the whole people were too heavy a burden for him. The Lord told Moses to choose seventy elders from the community and bring them before the Lord. Moses did as the Lord said, and the Lord gave part of the spirit he had given Moses to the seventy elders. In this way they shared Moses' responsibilities. The spirit touched them all, and they prophesied. Joshua asked Moses to stop their prophecies. Moses replied that he wished all the Lord's people were prophets, and that the Lord would give his spirit to them all.

Psalm 19 or 19:7–14

The psalmist praises God's law.

The Epistle James 4:7–12 (13—5:6)

God's law is a law of love, and Christians are not to judge one another. The wealthy merchants say, "Today or tomorrow we will go into a town and spend a year there, making money." They have no idea what tomorrow will bring for them, and they should be saying, "If it be the Lord's will, we will live, and we will do this or that."

The Gospel Mark 9:38–43, 45, 47–48

When Jesus' disciple John said to him, "Master, we saw a man driving out devils in your name, and since he wasn't one of us, we tried to stop him," Jesus told John to accept those people who tried to do good in his name, and above all to tear out without mercy those things in themselves that cause sin.

Year C

The Lesson   Amos 6:1–7

The message of the Lord, through the prophet Amos to the leaders of the House of Israel, was that they would be the first to go into exile. They had lived in ease and luxury, feasting and drinking; and this harsh prophecy foretold the capture of Hamath by the Assyrians.

Psalm 146 or 146:4–9

Praise to the Lord for his goodness to the poor and oppressed.

The Epistle   1 Timothy 6:11–19

Paul reminds Timothy of his calling to run the race of faith and take hold of eternal life. Paul charges Timothy to obey orders without fault until the coming of our Lord Jesus Christ. Timothy is to speak to those who are wealthy, and to tell them to fix their hopes on God rather than on money, to give away and to share, so that they may grasp the life which is truly life.

The Gospel   Luke 16:19–31

Jesus told a story of a very rich man and a poor man who was ill and lay hungry at the rich man's gate. He would have been grateful for the table scraps from the rich man's house, but not even that much mercy was shown to him. The poor man, who was called Lazarus, was carried by the angels to be with Abraham, and the rich man found himself in the torment of Hades. The rich man, who could see Lazarus with Abraham, begged Abraham to send Lazarus back to life to warn his five brothers. Abraham said that the brothers had already been warned by Moses and the prophets, and the rich man said that if someone came back from the dead to warn them, they would repent. Abraham replied that if they will not listen to Moses and the prophets, they would not be convinced even if someone were to rise from the dead.

Proper 22:

The Sunday closest to October 5
Themes of the Collect:

- God is always more ready to hear than we are to pray,
- and to give us more than we desire or deserve.
- We pray that he will show us mercy
- and forgive us the things our consciences are afraid of;
- and give us the good things we would not be worthy to ask if it were not for the mediation of Jesus Christ our Lord.

Year A

The Lesson   Isaiah 5:1–7

The prophet sings a song about a vineyard high on a fertile hillside, to which the owner had given every care. When it was time for the vineyard to produce grapes, its grapes were sour. The vineyard is Israel and the people of Israel the vines the Lord cherished. Nothing remains for the vineyard but destruction.

Psalm 80 or 80:7–14

The psalmist describes the people of Israel as a vine brought out of Egypt, and calls upon God to take thought for the vine and tend it.

The Epistle   Philippians 3:14–21

Paul urges the followers of Christ to lead lives according to the example he has set. He grieves for those whose minds are on earthly things and who are heading for destruction. Christians live as citizens of heaven from which our deliverer, the Lord Jesus Christ, will come.

The Gospel   Matthew 21:33–43

The Wicked Tenants. Jesus told another story to the chief priests and elders and others who were listening, about a landowner who planted a vineyard and rented it, and left that part of the country. At harvest time he sent some of his servants to collect his share of the fruit. The tenants seized his servants, beat one, killed another, and stoned a third. The landlord sent a larger number of servants who suffered the same treatment. So the owner sent his own son, saying, "They will respect my son." But when the tenants saw the son they said, "This is the heir. Let us kill him and take the vineyard." They threw the son out of the vineyard and killed him.

Jesus asked, "What will the owner of the vineyard do to those tenants?" They answered, "He will bring those wretches to a miserable death and will hand the vineyard over to tenants who will give him his share of the fruit."

Then Jesus said, "The Kingdom of God will be taken from you and given to a people who will produce its fruits."

The story is an allegory: The landowner is God; the vineyard is Israel; and the tenants are the people of Israel. The servants are the prophets, and the son is Jesus.

Year B

The Lesson   Genesis 2:18–24

The Lord God said, "It is not good that the man should be alone. I will make other living things to be with him," and from the earth God formed the beasts of the field and the birds of the air, and brought them to the man to see what he would call them. The man gave them all names, but still the man had no real companion. God made the man fall into a deep sleep, and from one of his ribs he made a woman, and brought her to the man. The man said, "This at last is bone from my bones and flesh from my flesh. She shall be called Woman, because she was taken out of Man." This is why a man leaves his father and mother and is with his wife, and the two become one. The man and woman were both naked, but were not ashamed in front of each other.

Psalm 8

A hymn of praise to God, whose power is acknowledged, and who made human beings who rule over all the creatures of the earth.

or Psalm 128

The Epistle   Hebrews 2:(1–8) 9–18

In v. 6–8 there is a quotation from Psalm 8. Because Christ has fully experienced human suffering and death, his sacrifice is all that is needed for our salvation.

The Gospel   Mark 10:2–9

Jesus was asked whether it was lawful for a man to divorce his wife, and Jesus referred the questioners to the law, which allows divorce. Jesus told them that God made that law for them because their hearts were closed. In the Creation God made people male and female. A man shall leave his parents and be one with his wife, and the two shall no longer be separate, but one flesh. What God has joined must not be separated.

Year C

The Lesson   Habakkuk 1:1–6 (7–11) 12–13—2:1–4

The prophet cries out to God for allowing lawlessness and violence to rule in Judah, and asks why God is silent. Habakkuk says he will stand on his watchtower and learn what God will say through him. God's answer comes: Habakkuk is to write down the vision so others may know it. If it seems slow, wait for it, the time will surely come. The righteous shall live by their faith.

Psalm 37:1–23 or 37:3–10

Wait patiently for the Lord; the righteous will be rewarded and the wicked will perish.

The Epistle   2 Timothy 1:(1–5) 6–14

After beginning with a prayer, Paul thanks God for the sincerity of Timothy's faith and urges Timothy to keep before him the sound teaching he has had, and to live by the faith and love that are ours in Jesus Christ.

The Gospel   Luke 17:5–10

When the disciples asked Jesus to increase their faith, he reminded them of the tremendous strength and power of faith. He went on to tell a story of a servant who worked all day in the fields, who must come back to the house and wait on his master before the servant can eat. The servant can expect no gratitude; and similarly when the disciples have carried out all their orders they are to say, "We are servants and deserve no credit; we have done our duty."

PROPER 23:

The Sunday closest to October 12
   Themes of the Collect:

   • We pray that God's grace will always go before us and follow us,

- and that we may be constantly alert to see need and to do good for others.

Year A

The Lesson   Isaiah 25:1–9

A hymn of thanksgiving for God's victory. God is the ultimate source of security; he is a refuge to the poor. He will give a great universal banquet in which God and man will live in communion. V.8 expresses hope for the end of death.

Psalm 23

The Lord is shepherd, host, and guide, present in time of danger. He spreads a feast of abundant blessing and joy for the one he watches over.

The Epistle   Philippians 4:4–13

Paul writes out of joyful faith and dedication to describe his inner peace and his relationship to others. Paul acknowledges the gift of the Philippians in sharing the burden of his troubles.

The Gospel   Matthew 22:1–14

There are two parables in this reading: The invitation to the wedding feast, and the wedding garment. The parable suggests that the Kingdom of God will become known whether people are ready for it or not. It is God's gift, and all sorts of people will be included, though many may not be worthy by the standards of the world.

The second parable reminds us that we must be ready for the King at all times. His invitation comes unexpectedly.

Year B

The Lesson   Amos 5:6–7, 10–15

The prophet tells of the sins of the people of Israel and of the punishment which God threatens. The possibility of life that is held out calls for genuinely seeking good and hating evil.

Psalm 90 or 90:1–8, 12

The psalmist describes the transitory nature of human life, and asks that the Lord will teach us to make the wisest use of the days that are given to us.

The Epistle   Hebrews 3:1–6

Christ is the mediator between God and people. He is more to be honored than Moses, who was a servant in God's household, while Christ is the Son of the Master. We are part of that household, if we hope and trust in our salvation.

The Gospel   Mark 10:17–27 (28–31)

A stranger ran up and knelt before Jesus, asking, "Good Master, what must I do to inherit eternal life?" Jesus told him that no one is *good* except God. Jesus reviewed the commandments, and the man said he had kept all these since he was young. Jesus responded warmly to the man and said, "You lack one thing. Sell everything you have and give it to the poor. You will have riches in heaven. Come, follow me." The man went away sadly, because he had great wealth.

Jesus said to his disciples that it will be very hard for people of wealth to enter the Kingdom of God. They were astonished and asked one another, "Who can be saved?" Jesus said, "For human beings it is impossible; but not with God, for with God everything is possible."

Year C

The Lesson   Ruth 1:(1–7) 8–19a

A man named Elimalech from Bethlehem in Judah went to live in Moabite country with his wife Naomi and their two sons. The sons married Moabite women called Orpah and Ruth. The father died and later both sons died also. Naomi decided to go home, because there was a famine and she had heard that the Lord was caring for his people in Judah. Naomi kissed her daughters-in-law and wished them well and told them to return to their own people. Orpah did go back to her parents' home; but Ruth would not leave in spite of Naomi's urging. Ruth said, "Where you go I will go, nothing but death shall divide us." Naomi realized that Ruth was determined to stay with her, and the two went on together until they arrived in Bethlehem. (This is how Ruth, who was King David's grandmother, came to Bethlehem.)

Psalm 113

A song of praise to the Lord, whose throne is high but who sees the lives of humble people and who makes the woman in a childless house the happy mother of children.

The Epistle   2 Timothy 2:(3–7) 8–15

Paul writes from prison, reminding Timothy that even though he is wearing chains like a criminal, the word of God is free. He urges Timothy to continue to proclaim the glorious salvation in Christ Jesus and to work to be worthy of God's approval, and to be forthright in speaking the truth.

The Gospel   Luke 17:11–19

Jesus was on the border roads between Samaria and Galilee. Ten lepers came from one of the villages to meet him. They stood at a distance and called, "Jesus, Master! take pity on us." Jesus told them to go and show themselves to the priests. As they went to do as he said, they were healed. One of the men, finding that he was cured, turned back, praising God in a loud voice. He fell at Jesus' feet and thanked him. This man was from Samaria. Jesus asked, "Weren't there ten who were cured? Where are the other nine? No one returned to praise God but this foreigner." Jesus said to the Samaritan, "Stand up and go your way. Your faith has made you well."

PROPER 24:

The Sunday closest to October 19
Themes of the Collect:

- God has shown his glory among the nations in Christ.
- We pray that God will preserve the works of his mercy
- so that his Church throughout the world may continue faithfully to confess his Name.

Year A

The Lesson   Isaiah 45:1–7

The Lord says that he will ransom Israel through his chosen representative, Cyrus, a foreign king. God himself leads Cyrus so that he will not fail to carry out his task.

Psalm 96 or 96:1–9

A new song of praise to the Lord, in which the families of nations are invited to join.

The Epistle   1 Thessalonians 1:1–10

Paul, Sylvanus, and Timothy write to the congregation in Thessalonica, giving thanks for a new and fruitful ministry. Everywhere the faith of this congregation is being praised; how they turned from idol worship to be servants of the living God and wait expectantly for the coming of his son Jesus.

The Gospel   Matthew 22:15–22

The Pharisees sent some of their people and some men of Herod's party to Jesus with a question intended to trap Jesus in his own words. They said, "Master, you are an honest man and you teach God's way truthfully, without considering the position of any man. Are we or are we not permitted to pay taxes to the Emperor of Rome?"

Jesus was aware of the malice in their question, and asked to see the money in which the tax was paid. They handed him a coin, and he asked, "Whose picture is this, and whose words are on the coin?" They answered, "Caesar's." Jesus said, "Pay Caesar what is due to Caesar, and pay God what is due to God." The reply surprised them and they went away.

Year B

The Lesson   Isaiah 53:4–12

Part of the fourth servant song, in which Israel, the servant of God, suffers as an individual who has been shamefully insulted; but the servant endures the suffering uncomplainingly, because it is suffering for others.

Psalm 91 or 91:9–16

A song of trust in God's protection over those who ask him for safety and shelter.

The Epistle   Hebrews 4:12–16

The word of God is alive, piercing and judging his whole Creation. But we do not have to be afraid to approach God, because Jesus, our great high priest, understands our weakness and has been tested in every way. He resisted all the temptations without sin. Through Christ we may receive help and mercy.

The Gospel Mark 10:35–45

James and John asked Jesus for the privilege of sitting in state at his right and left when he came into his Kingdom. Jesus told them that they didn't know what they were asking. They could drink from the cup from which Jesus drank, and they could be baptized with the same baptism; but what they asked was not for Jesus to grant. The other disciples were angry at James and John; and Jesus called them to him and said that those who rule the Gentiles exert great authority over their people, but it is not to be so among the disciples. Whoever would be great must be a servant, because the Son of Man had not come to be served but to serve, and to give his life as a ransom for many.

Year C

The Lesson Genesis 32:3–8, 22–30

After Jacob had worked for Laban for twenty years, Jacob sent messengers to his brother Esau that he had been with Laban all this time and now owned substantial property. The messengers returned saying that they had seen Esau and he was on his way to meet Jacob, bringing four hundred men with him. Jacob was frightened because of what he had done to his brother years before and he divided his people and flocks into two groups and sent them out, and only Jacob was left in the camp.

A stranger came in the darkness and wrestled with Jacob. When the stranger saw he couldn't win, he struck Jacob on the hip, and Jacob's hip was out of joint. The stranger said, "It is daybreak. Let me go." Jacob said, "I will not let you go unless you bless me." The stranger asked Jacob's name and Jacob told him. The stranger said, "Your name shall no longer be Jacob but Israel. You have held fast to God and to men and have been victorious." Jacob asked the stranger's name, and the stranger said, "Why do you ask my name?" and blessed Jacob. Jacob called the place Peniel, because "I have seen God face to face, and yet I am alive."

Psalm 121

The Lord is the guardian of Israel who never sleeps, and who guards his people now and forever.

The Epistle 2 Timothy 3:14—4:5

Paul tells Timothy to remember from whom he learned the truths of the faith; and to proclaim the message, to use every gift at his command, and to teach with the necessary patience. The time will come when his hearers turn from the truth to mythology. But Timothy must keep calm, face the hardships, and work for the spread of the Gospel.

The Gospel Luke 18:1–8a
In order to show his disciples that they were to keep on praying and never to lose heart, Jesus told a parable of a judge who didn't fear God and who cared nothing for men. There was a widow who came to him constantly, demanding justice against her opponent. For a time the judge refused, and at last he said to himself, "This widow is a great bother. I will decide in her favor before she wears me out with her persistence." Jesus said, "You hear what the judge said. Will not God hear the prayers of his chosen when they cry out to him?" God doesn't have to be worn down by continual persistent pleading like the unrighteous judge; but the Righteous Judge will surely hear the prayers of his chosen.

PROPER 25:

The Sunday closest to October 26
Themes of the Collect:

- We pray that God will increase in us the gifts of faith, hope, and love
- and that he will make us love what he commands,
- so that we may receive what he promises.

Year A

The Lesson Exodus 22:21–27
As part of their covenant with the Lord God, the people of Israel are sternly forbidden to wrong strangers; they had themselves been foreigners in Egypt. If they ill-treat widows or fatherless children, the Lord will listen to the appeals of the widows and orphans and he will be angry, and their wives will become widows and their children fatherless. There were also severe prohibitions against exacting interest from the poor. The Lord is on the side of the poor and oppressed.

Psalm 1

The psalmist points out the two ways of life open to people, good and evil, and the consequences.

The Epistle   1 Thessalonians 2:1–8

Paul, Sylvanus, and Timothy write of their earlier visit, of the hostility they had experienced at Philippi, and the difficulties in Thessalonica. They speak of their frank and fearless preaching of the Gospel in those places, and their affection for the congregation at Thessalonica.

The Gospel   Matthew 22:34–46

One of the Pharisees asked Jesus a test question: "Which is the greatest commandment in the law?" Jesus answered, "You shall love the Lord your God with all your heart and with all your soul and with all your mind. This is the first and great commandment, and a second is like it. You shall love your neighbor as yourself. All the law and the prophets depend on these two commandments." Then Jesus asked the Pharisees a question: "What do you think about the Messiah? Whose son is he?" "The son of David," they answered. "If David calls him Lord, how can he be David's son?" Jesus asked, and none of his questioners could say a word in reply.

Year B

The Lesson   Isaiah 59:(1–4) 9–19

The prophet describes the sins of Israel, the acts of rebellion are countless, evil is rampant. The Lord is the High God of retribution, he will pay in full measure, and he will come as the ransomer of Zion and of all who repent of their rebellion.

Psalm 13

The psalmist cries, "How long, O Lord . . .?" He has a request to make, he affirms his trust, and closes with a promise that he will sing to the Lord, who has granted all his wishes.

The Epistle   Hebrews 5:12—6:1, 9–12

Those to whom the letter is sent have needed the milk of basic understanding in distinguishing between good and evil; but now, with the foundations of faith, repentance, resurrection, and judgment, they are to advance toward maturity, if God permits. God will not forget the work and love they continue to show in service, and they are to go on in the way of life of those who, through faith and patience, inherit the promise.

Jesus and his disciples were leaving Jericho, followed by a great crowd. Bartimaeus, a blind beggar sitting beside the road, began to cry out, "Son of David, have mercy on me!" Jesus stopped and said, "Call him." They called Bartimaeus, saying, "Take heart. Stand up, he's calling you!" Bartimaeus threw aside his cloak and sprang up and came to Jesus, who asked, "What do you want me to do for you?" The blind man said, "Master, let me receive my sight." Jesus said, "Go your way. Your faith has made you whole." Bartimaeus recovered his sight, and followed Jesus on the road.

Year C

The Lesson   Jeremiah 14:(1–6) 7–10, 19–22
The word of the Lord concerning the terrible drought in Judah came to Jeremiah. The people cry to the Lord for relief and make public confession of their sins.

Psalm 84 or 84:1–6
The psalmist praises the temple of the Lord and rejoices in the water the Lord sends.

The Epistle   2 Timothy 4:6–8, 16–18
Paul, who is in prison in Rome, thinks that the end of his life will come soon, and writes to Timothy, secure in the knowledge that his rewards are waiting for him. His friends did not stand by him in his trouble, but the Lord gave Paul strength to preach the Gospel, and rescued him from the lion's jaws. The Lord will continue to be with Paul and keep him safe until the Lord's heavenly reign begins.

The Gospel   Luke 18:9–14
Jesus told a parable to some people who were self-satisfied about their righteousness and looked down on others. "Two men went to the temple to pray, one a Pharisee (a religious man) and the other a tax collector (an outcast). The Pharisee stood and prayed, "God, I thank you that I am not like other men who are extortioners, unjust, adulterers, or like this

tax collector. I fast twice a week and I give tithes of all I get.'' The tax collector, standing far away, didn't even raise his eyes to heaven. He beat his breast, saying, ''God be merciful to me, a sinner.'' Jesus said that it was the tax collector who went home justified rather than the Pharisee. Everyone who exalts himself will be humbled; but the one who humbles himself will be exalted.

PROPER 26:

The Sunday closest to November 2
   Themes of the Collect:

- It is only through the gift of God's grace that his faithful people offer him true and worthy service.
- We ask that we may go forward without falling to receive God's promises of eternal life.

Year A

The Lesson   Micah 3:5–12
   The false prophets who make promises in return for the money and favors of their employers will get no answer from God. Justice is for sale; priests take bribes; and yet the people rely upon the Lord. Because of the sins of the leaders, Zion shall become a plowed field, Jerusalem a heap of ruins, and the hill of the temple will be overgrown with trees.

Psalm 43
   The psalmist cries for God's help. He longs to be guided to the temple, where he may worship and praise God.

The Epistle   1 Thessalonians 2:9–13, 17–20
   Paul did not usually accept support from the churches he established. He worked for a living so as not to be dependent upon anyone. Paul rejoices that the congregation at Thessalonica received God's message as what it truly is, the Word of God at work in those who hold the faith. Paul had wanted more than once to return to Thessalonica to see the congregation again, but he speaks of being hindered by Satan. The Christians in Thessalonica are his glory and joy.

The Gospel   Matthew 23:1–12

Jesus tells his disciples that the learned doctors of the law and the Pharisees have the authority of Moses, therefore the disciples must pay attention to their words; but the disciples must not do as the leaders do, for they do not practice what they preach. They love the places of honor, the best seats in the synagogues, and the titles of honor by which they are called. The disciples are to have no titles and to use no titles in addressing others; they have one teacher and they are all brothers. The greatest among the disciples must be the servant of all, and the person who exalts himself will be humbled.

Year B

The Lesson   Deuteronomy 6:1–9

Moses tells the people that they must keep the commandments which he gives them constantly in their hearts and before them as they live through each day. They are to teach the commandments to their children, and write them on the doors and gates of their homes. If Israel listens and observes the commandments, they will prosper and increase as God has promised.

Psalm 119:1–16 or 119:1–8

Those people who faithfully keep God's commandments are truly fortunate.

The Epistle   Hebrews 7:23–28

The priesthood of Jesus is forever, and he is able to save those who draw near to God through him, because he lives to intercede for them. He has no need to offer daily sacrifice. He did this once and for all when he sacrificed his own life. The word of the oath, which came later than the law, appoints a Son who has been made perfect forever.

The Gospel   Mark 12:28–34

One of the lawyers who had been listening to Jesus asked him, "Which commandment is first of all?" Jesus answered, "The first is, 'Hear, O Israel: The Lord our God, the Lord is one, and you shall love the Lord your God with all your heart, and with all your soul, and with all your mind, and with all your strength.' The second is, 'You shall love your neighbor as yourself.' There are no greater commandments.'' The lawyer said, ''You are right, Teacher. To fulfill these commandments is far more than burnt offerings or sacrifices.'' Jesus was moved by the lawyer's thoughtful answer and said, ''You are not far from the Kingdom of God.''

Year C

The Lesson   Isaiah 1:10–20

The prophet Isaiah speaks the Word of the Lord to the rulers of Israel, who are so wicked that they are compared to the cities of Sodom and Gomorrah. Their countless sacrifices, their sacred seasons and ceremonies, and their endless prayers are abhorrent to the Lord. He asks them to stop doing evil, and to be just. As wicked as the rulers have been, they may be forgiven if they will obey. If they rebel, they will be punished.

Psalm 32 or 32:1–8

A song of thanksgiving for the forgiveness of sin.

The Epistle   2 Thessalonians 1:1–5 (6–10) 11–12

Paul, Sylvanus, and Timothy write to the congregation of Thessalonians, thanking God for their increasing faith and love in the face of the troubles they endure. The persecutions will prove them worthy of the Kingdom of God, for which they are suffering.

The Gospel   Luke 19:1–10

The chief tax collector in Jericho was a rich man named Zacchaeus. He was eager to see Jesus but he wasn't tall enough to look over the crowd, so he ran ahead and climbed into a sycamore tree. When Jesus passed the tree he looked up and said, ''Zacchaeus, come down quickly, because I must stay at your house today.'' Zacchaeus climbed down and welcomed Jesus joyfully. There was a disapproving murmur, ''He has gone to be the guest of a sinner.'' Zacchaeus said to the Lord, ''Half of my goods I will give to the poor, and if I have cheated anyone I am ready to repay him four times over.'' Jesus said, ''Salvation has come to this house today. This man is also a son of Abraham, and the Son of Man has come to look for and to save what is lost.''

The Sunday closest to November 9
  Themes of the Collect:

- God's Son came into the world to destroy the works of the devil
- and to make us children of God and heirs of eternal life.
- Since we have this hope, we pray that we may make ourselves pure as he is pure,
- and when he comes again with power and great glory,
- we may be made like him in his eternal and glorious Kingdom.

Year A

The Lesson   Amos 5:18–24
  The prophet Amos warns that the day of the Lord will be a day of gloom with no dawn. The Lord rejects the feasts and ceremonies of the people of Israel. Justice must roll like a river, and righteousness like an everflowing stream.

Psalm 70
  A cry for help from one who is poor and needy to the God of salvation.

The Epistle   1 Thessalonians 4:13–18
  Paul writes to the congregation at Thessalonica to explain that they should not grieve for those who have died as Christians. They will rise to life with Jesus. Paul's vision of the coming of Christ is dramatic, and it carries as a climax, ". . . so we shall always be with the Lord."

The Gospel   Matthew 25:1–13
  Jesus told a parable based on the wedding customs of the day to show the need for preparedness for the coming of the Kingdom. He said that the Kingdom of heaven will be like ten maidens who took their lamps and went to meet the bridegroom. There were five who took no oil for their lamps. The five who used forethought took flasks of oil.
  The bridegroom was late, and all the maidens went to sleep. At midnight a cry was heard, "Come out and meet the bridegroom!" All the maidens got up and adjusted their lamps. The foolish maidens said, "Our lamps are going out. Give us some of your oil." Those who had

brought the oil said there would not be enough for all the lamps; the five had better buy some. While they were away the bridegroom came, and those who were ready went in to the wedding, and the door was closed. When the five came back, they cried, "Lord! Lord! open the door for us!" He replied, "Truly, I do not know you." And Jesus added, "Watch, because you never know the day or the hour."

Year B

The Lesson   1 Kings 17:8–16
  In a time of severe drought, the word of the Lord came to Elijah: He was to stay at Zarephath, where the Lord had commanded a widow to feed him. When Elijah reached the village he saw a widow gathering sticks and asked her for water and a piece of bread. She said the only food she had was a handful of flour and a little oil. She was gathering the sticks to make something for her son and herself to eat before they died. Elijah told her to make a little cake from what she had and bring it to him; and then make something for her son and herself. The God of Israel had promised that the jar of flour should not give out nor the flask of oil be empty until the Lord sent rain to the land. The woman did as Elijah said, and there was food for them all for a long time.

Psalm 146 or 146:4–9
  A song of praise to the Lord, who feeds the hungry, frees the prisoner, restores sight to the blind, and provides for the orphan and the widow.

The Epistle   Hebrews 9:24–28
  Christ has not entered a sanctuary made by human hands, which is only a symbol of the reality; but heaven itself, where he appears before God on our behalf. He came once and for all to abolish sin by the sacrifice of himself. Men die once, and after death comes judgment; Christ was offered once to bear the burden of men's sins, and will appear again to bring salvation to those who are waiting for him.

The Gospel   Mark 12:38–44
  Jesus was teaching a large crowd of eager listeners. He said, "Beware of the doctors of the law who walk about in long robes and are greeted with respect. They have the chief seats in synagogues and the places of honor at feasts. They eat up the property of widows while they say long

prayers as a pretense. They will be severely judged." Jesus sat down opposite the temple treasury watching as people dropped money into the chest. Many rich people put in large sums. A poor widow came by and put in two small copper coins worth a penny. He called his disciples and said: "This poor widow has given more than any of the others. They gave out of their affluence, but she, out of her poverty, put in all that she had to live on."

Year C

The Lesson   Job 19:23–27a
Job describes wrongs done him by his friends. He wishes his words could be engraved in rock so that he could be judged by others. He knows that his Redeemer lives, and he will at last be vindicated.

Psalm 17 or 17:1–8
The psalmist calls on the Lord for justice and help.

The Epistle   2 Thessalonians 2:13—3:5
Paul, Sylvanus, and Timothy thank God for the congregation at Thessalonica because God called them through the Gospel so that they might possess for their own the glory of the Lord Jesus Christ. They are to stand firm and hold fast to what they have learned. Paul asks them to pray that the Word of the Lord may speed on and triumph everywhere as it has with them; and to pray that Paul and his companions will be safe from evil men.

The Gospel   Luke 20:27 (28–33) 34–38
Some Sadducees, who denied that there is a resurrection, described a situation to Jesus: A man who was the oldest of seven brothers died, and each of his brothers, fulfilling the law that says the next son shall marry the widow and carry on his brother's family, married the widow, and in turn, each died. Whose wife would the widow be at the resurrection, since she had been the wife of all seven?

Jesus replied that the people who share in the resurrection do not marry; they are children of God and no longer subject to death. God is not God of the dead, but of the living; for him all are alive.

The Sunday closest to November 16
Themes of the Collect:

- God caused all holy Scripture to be written for our learning.
- We ask that we may hear, read, take careful notice of, learn, and make the Scriptures our own,
- so that we may hold fast the blessed hope of eternal life.

Year A

The Lesson   Zephaniah 1:7, 12–18
   The prophet Zephaniah pronounces doom on Judah and the neighboring countries, a day of wrath when the Lord will make a swift end of all who live in the earth.

Psalm 90 or 90:1–8, 12
   The psalmist speaks of the power of God's wrath and of the shortness of life. He prays for wisdom.

The Epistle   1 Thessalonians 5:1–10
   Paul, Sylvanus, and Timothy writing to the church at Thessalonica, remind them that the Day of the Lord Jesus Christ will come unexpectedly. They are to live in faith and love, knowing that God has not destined them for the terrors of his wrath but to receive salvation through Jesus Christ who died so that his true followers, alive or dead, may live in company with him.

The Gospel   Matthew 25:14–15, 19–29
   Jesus told a parable of the Kingdom of God, saying that it was like a man who was going abroad and who put his wealth into the hands of his servants, giving them different sums of money. When the master returned, one servant, who had been trusted with five talents (an ancient measure of money) brought out five more. His master was delighted and said that since the servant had been trustworthy over a comparatively small sum he would be given charge of a great deal. The second servant,

who had been given two talents, and had two more for his master, was given similar approval. The third servant was afraid of his master, and when the master returned he brought the one talent he had been given, saying that he had buried the talent and brought it back safely. The master was angry, and said the servant should have put the money out at interest so that there would be an increase when the master returned. The talent was taken from this servant and given to the one with the ten talents.

Year B

The Lesson   Daniel 12:1–4a (5–13)
   Daniel has a vision of the end of time, when Michael, the angel of Israel, who is described as a great captain, will appear and the people will be delivered. Some will wake to everlasting life and some to eternal humiliation. Daniel is to keep secret the names in the book of life until the end of the age.

Psalm 16 or 16:5–11
   The Lord will watch over his faithful servant and show him the path of life.

The Epistle   Hebrews 10:31–39
   "It is a terrible thing to fall into the hands of the living God." In earlier days, when the readers were new Christians, they patiently endured great hardships and suffering for the sake of their faith. Now they must be confident and endure, for it will not be long. Christians are not among those who shrink back and are lost; they have faith to choose life.

The Gospel   Mark 13:14–23
   Jesus warns the disciples of false signs and wonders, and false Messiahs and prophets who will arise in a time of terrible affliction to come.

Year C

The Lesson   Malachi 3:13—4:2a, 5–6
   There were those who said, "It is useless to serve God. It is the evildoers who prosper." The Lord knows those who obey him and keep his name in honor, and they are his own. In his day, and in his way, the

good will be divided from the bad. God will send the prophet Elijah before the great and terrible day of the Lord comes. He will reconcile parents and children, for fear that the Lord will destroy the land.

Psalm 98 or 98:5–10
The psalmist sings to the Lord, who will come with power and establish justice.

The Epistle 2 Thessalonians 3:6–13
Because they believe that the age in which they live will not continue, and that they themselves are above ordinary obligations, some Christians are living in idleness. When Paul was with them he gave the Christian community a rule: Those who will not work shall not eat. Paul appeals to the idle ones in the name of the Lord Jesus Christ to work quietly to earn their living; and he charges every one never to tire of doing right.

The Gospel Luke 21:5–19
Some people were talking about the Temple, its fine stones and adornments. Jesus said, "The time is coming when not one of the stones you are looking at will be left standing." They asked him, "Master, what will be the sign that this is about to happen?" Jesus said, "Don't be misled, because many will come claiming my name and saying that the Day has come. Don't be frightened when you hear of wars and revolutions, these things will happen first. But before all the terrible disasters come, people will persecute you for your loyalty to me. Even those closest to you will betray you and some of you will be put to death. You will be hated for your faithfulness to me; but you will not be harmed. Stand firm, and you will win true life."

PROPER 29:

The Sunday closest to November 23
Themes of the Collect:

- It is God's will to restore all things in Jesus Christ, who is King of kings and Lord of lords.
- The people of the earth are divided from one another and dominated by sin.
- We pray that God will free the people and unify them under the gracious rule of our Lord Jesus Christ.

Year A

The Lesson   Ezekiel 34:11–17

The Lord will be the Shepherd of his people. He will find them, no matter where they are, and bring them home. He will feed them in rich pastures, and the Lord himself will tend his flock. The Lord God says to his flock, "I will judge between one sheep and another."

Psalm 95:1–7

A joyful song to the Lord who is the Rock of our salvation. He is our God, and we are his sheep.

The Epistle   1 Corinthians 15:20–28

Paul writes of the resurrection, saying that Christ has been truly raised to life. As all men die, so in Christ all will be brought to life. Christ is destined to reign until God has put all enemies under his feet, and the final enemy to be done away with is death.

The Gospel   Matthew 25:31–46

Jesus describes the Judgment, when the Son of Man will come in glory and all the people will be gathered before him. He will divide the people into two groups. He will welcome those on his right hand to the Kingdom that has been ready for them since the world began, because they fed him when he was hungry, gave him something to drink when he was thirsty, took him into their homes when he was a stranger, clothed him when he was naked, and visited him in prison. The people on his right hand will ask when they had done these things and the King will answer that anything they did for the humblest of his brothers was done for the King.

He will send those on the left to eternal fire because when he was in need they did not help. And they also will ask, "Lord, when did we see you suffering and do nothing for you?" And the King will answer, "Anything you did not do for one of these, however humble, you did not do for me." They will go to eternal punishment while the righteous enter eternal life.

Year B

The Lesson   Daniel 7:9–14

Daniel had a dream, and wrote it down. He had strange visions; and

Daniel looked and saw thrones, where one who was ancient of days took his seat. As the visions continued, Daniel saw a man surrounded by the clouds of heaven approach the Ancient of Days (God). Sovereignty and glory and kingly power were given to the man, all people and nations should serve him. His everlasting sovereignty will not pass away, and his kingly power will never be destroyed.

Psalm 93
The Lord is King of his Creation. His throne is everlasting.

The Epistle Revelation 1:1–8
The revelation given to John, a disciple, is sent to the seven churches in Asia. It opens with a greeting from God, who is, and was, and is to come; from the seven spirits before God's throne; and from Jesus Christ, who was faithful to his death. Jesus Christ is coming with the clouds. Every eye shall see him; everyone who pierced him and all the peoples of the world shall cry out in remorse. "I am the first and last, Alpha and Omega, the Almighty," says the Lord God.

The Gospel John 18:33–37
Pilate, the Roman governor, asked Jesus, "Are you the King of the Jews?" Jesus answered with a question, "Do you say this, or did others say it to you about me?" Pilate said, "Am I a Jew? Your own people and chief priests have brought you before me. What have you done?" Jesus replied, "My Kingdom does not belong to this world. My kingly authority comes from elsewhere." Pilate said, "So you are a king?" and Jesus answered, "You say that I am a king. I was born, and I have come into the world, to bear witness to the truth. Everyone who is of the truth hears my voice."

or Mark 11:1–11

Year C

The Lesson Jeremiah 23:1–6
Shame on the shepherds (rulers) who let the sheep of my flock scatter and be lost! These are the words of the Lord God of Israel about the shepherds who tend my people. You have not watched over my flock, and I am watching you to punish you for your evil doings. I will gather

the remnant of my sheep and bring them home. I will appoint shepherds to tend them, and they shall never again suffer fear or dismay or punishment.

The Lord says: The days are coming when I will appoint a truly righteous King to rule in Israel, a Branch of David's line. He shall be called "The Lord is our Righteousness."

Psalm 46

A hymn to God's power: The Lord of Hosts is with us, the God of Jacob is our stronghold.

The Epistle Colossians 1:11–20

Paul prays that God will strengthen the people of the church at Colossae to meet whatever may come to them with fortitude, patience, joy, and thankfulness to God. Christ is the image of the invisible God; all things were created through him or for him. He is the head of the body, the church, and its origin. God chose to reconcile all things to himself through Christ, making peace through the shedding of his blood on the cross.

The Gospel Luke 25:35–43

The people watched and the rulers scoffed at Jesus: "He saved others, let him save himself if he is God's Messiah, his Chosen." The soldiers mocked Jesus, too, and offered him sour wine, saying, "If you are the King of the Jews, save yourself." One of the criminals who had been crucified with Jesus taunted him, asking, "Are you not the Messiah? Save yourself and us." The other criminal said, "Do you not fear God? You are under the same sentence as he is, and for us it is justice, because we are paying the consequences of our actions, but this man has done nothing wrong." He said, "Jesus, remember me when you come in your kingly power." Jesus answered, "Today you will be with me in paradise."

or Luke 19:29–38

SUMMARY OF THE PSALMS AND LESSONS FOR THE FEAST
OF THE PRESENTATION

Themes of the Collect (BCP 187, 239):

- The Son of God was this day presented in the temple.
- We pray to be presented to God with pure and clean hearts by Jesus Christ.

Years A, B, C

The Lesson   Malachi 3:1–4
The prophet proclaims the future coming of the Lord to his temple, when he will purify the priests and the offerings.

Psalm 84:1–6
A song of thanksgiving for the temple. "How dear to me is your dwelling, O Lord of hosts!"

The Epistle   Hebrews 2:14–18
Jesus Christ partook of our human nature, so that as high priest he could make expiation for our sins. Since he himself had suffered and been tempted, he can help us, who also suffer and are tempted.

The Gospel   Luke 2:22–40
In fulfillment of the Law, Mary and Joseph bring the infant Jesus to the temple to present him to the Lord. The righteous Simeon, who has been promised that he will see the messiah before he dies, takes Jesus in his arms, blesses him, and says, "Lord, now lettest thou thy servant depart in peace, according to thy word; for mine eyes have seen thy salvation . . ." Anna, a prophetess, also sees Jesus and speaks of the coming redemption.

SUMMARY OF PSALMS AND LESSONS FOR THE SERVICES ON INDEPENDENCE DAY

JULY 4

Themes of the Collect (BCP 190, 242):
- The founders of this country won liberty for themselves and for us in the name of Almighty God,
- and lit the torch of freedom for nations then unborn.
- Grant that we and all the people of this land may have grace to maintain our liberties in righteousness and peace.
- The Collect "For the Nation," (BCP 207 or 258) may be used instead.

All Years

The Lesson   Deuteronomy 10:17–21
    Moses said to the people of Israel: The Lord your God secures justice for widows and orphans; he loves the foreigners who live among you. You also must love the foreigner, because you were foreigners in Egypt. You must fear God, serve him, hold fast to him, and take your oaths in his name. He is your praise, your God, who has done these great and terrible things you have seen with your own eyes.

Psalm 145 or 145:1–9
    A hymn praising the goodness and greatness of God.

The Epistle   Hebrews 11:8–16
    By faith Abraham obeyed a call to go to an unknown land intended for him and his heirs. By faith he lived there as a stranger, and by faith Issac and Jacob lived there also. Abraham looked forward to the city with firm foundations whose builder is God. By faith Sarah received power to conceive a child, though she was past the age. From one man was born a multitude of descendants, all of whom died in faith, knowing themselves to be strangers and exiles on earth, longing for a better country, a heavenly country. That is why God is not ashamed to be called their God because he has a city ready for them.

The Gospel   Matthew 5:43–48

Jesus told his disciples, "You have heard it said 'You shall love your neighbor and hate your enemy.' But I tell you, love your enemies and pray for your persecutors, so that you may be children of your heavenly Father who makes the sun rise and the rain fall on good and bad alike. If you love only those who love you, even the tax collectors do as much as that. There must be no limit to your goodness as there is no limit to the goodness of your heavenly Father."

The Psalm and Lessons "For the Nation" (BCP 930) may be used instead.

SUMMARY OF THE PSALMS AND LESSONS FOR THE FEAST OF THE TRANSFIGURATION

AUGUST 6

Themes of the Collect (BCP 191, 243):

- God revealed his Son to chosen witnesses on the mountain.
- We pray that we too may behold the King in his beauty.

Years A, B, C

The Lesson   Exodus 34:29–35

Moses, having spoken with the Lord on Mount Sinai, must veil his face when he speaks to the people, since his skin is shining.

Psalm 99:5–9

A proclamation of God's greatness. "He spoke to them out of the pillar of cloud. . . . Proclaim the greatness of the Lord our God and worship him upon his holy hill. . . ."

The Epistle   II Peter 1:13–21

A reminiscence of the Transfiguration as by an eyewitness.

The Gospel   Luke 9:28–36

Jesus takes Peter, John, and James with him into the mountain. While he is praying, his countenance changes and his clothing becomes dazzlingly white. Moses and Elijah appear and speak with him. Peter, not knowing what he is saying, proposes that they construct three booths: one for Jesus, one for Moses, and one for Elijah. A voice from the cloud says, "This is my Son, my Chosen; listen to him!" After the voice has spoken, Jesus is alone with the disciples.

SUMMARY OF THE PSALMS AND LESSONS FOR THE SERVICES OF ALL SAINTS' DAY

NOVEMBER I

Themes of the Collect (BCP 194, 245):

- God has knit together his chosen in one communion and fellowship in the mystical body of his Son Jesus Christ our Lord.
- We pray that God will give us grace to follow his blessed saints in virtuous and godly living
- so that we may come to those indescribable joys he has prepared for those who truly love him.

All Years

The Lesson   Ecclesiasticus 44:1–10, 13–14

"Let us now praise famous men, and our fathers in their generations." We remember those who have gone before because they reveal God's majesty and glory. These were merciful people whose righteous work has not been forgotten. Their names will live to all generations.

or Ecclesiasticus 2 (1–6), 7–11

Psalm 149

The psalmist sings a new song to the Lord, who accepts the services of his people and crowns the humble with victory.

The Epistle   Revelation 7:2–4, 9–17

A vision of a multitude from every nation, of all tribes and peoples and tongues, standing before the throne of God, and praising God. These are the people who have passed through the great ordeal, whose robes have been washed white in the blood of the Lamb. They shall never again suffer hunger or thirst or scorching heat; the Lamb will be their shepherd and guide; and God will wipe all tears from their eyes.

or Ephesians 1 (11–14) 15–23

The Gospel   Matthew 5:1–12

The opening words of the Sermon on the Mount in which Jesus teaches that the Kingdom of Heaven belongs to those who know their need of God, the sorrowful, the meek, those who hunger and thirst for righteousness, the merciful, the pure in heart, the peacemakers, and the persecuted.

or Luke 6:20–26 (27–36)

SUMMARY OF PSALMS AND LESSONS FOR THANKSGIVING DAY

Themes of Collect (BCP 149, 246):

- We give thanks to God for the fruits of the earth in their season,
- and for the work of those who harvest them.
- We pray that we may be faithful stewards of God's great bounty to us,
- to provide for our necessities and for the relief of all who are in need.

For the Prayers of the People, the Litany of Thanksgiving (BCP 836) may be used.

All Years

The Lesson   Deuteronomy 8:1–3, 6–10 (17–20)

Moses said to the people of Israel: You must be careful to do everything I command you today, so that you may live and increase in the land the Lord promised to your forefathers. God is bringing you to a rich land, where you will never want for anything. You will bless the Lord for the land he has given you.

You must not say to yourselves, "My own strength and energy have gained me this wealth." Remember that it is the Lord your God who gives you the power to get wealth.

Psalm 65 or 65:9–14
A hymn of thanksgiving, praising God for the ways in which he visits the earth and crowns the year with his goodness.

The Epistle   James 1:17–18, 21–27
Every good and every perfect gift comes from the Father of the lights of heaven. By declaring the truth he brought us forth to be a kind of first fruits of his creatures. Act on the message God has planted in your hearts; don't be just a listener. Religion that is pure and faultless in the sight of God is to help orphans and widows in their trouble and need; and to keep oneself unstained from the world.

The Gospel   Matthew 6:25–33
Jesus said, "I tell you, do not be anxious about your life, about food and drink, or clothes to wear. Life is more than food and your body more than clothes. The birds do not sow or reap or store in barns, and yet your heavenly Father feeds them. Set your mind on God's kingdom and his justice; everything else will come to you."